HECATE
THE GODDESS OF WITCHCRAFT

GREGORY LEE WHITE

White Willow Press
Nashville, TN

Hecate – The Goddess of Witchcraft
by
Gregory Lee White

Text:
Gregory Lee White

Cover Art:
Gregory Lee White
based on the triple goddess version of Hecate found in many statues across the
centuries, sometimes called the triformis Hecate.

Interior Illustrations:
various artists and illustrators from 1890 to the 2000s

First Edition 2025

Published by
White Willow Press
211 Donelson Pike, Suite 111
Nashville, Tn 37214

Printed in the United States

ISBN: 978-1-965586-05-1

TABLE OF CONTENTS

OTHER BOOKS BY GREGORY LEE WHITE

Clucked – The Tale of Pickin Chicken

Making Soap from Scratch: How to Make Handmade Soap – A Beginners Guide and Beyond

Essential Oils and Aromatherapy - How to Use Essential Oils for Beauty, Health, and Spirituality

Little House Search – A Puzzle Book and Tour of the Works of Laura
Ingalls Wilder

The Use of Magical Oils in Hoodoo, Prayer, and Spellwork

Papa Gee's Hoodoo Herbal - The Magic of Herbs, Roots, and Minerals in the Hoodoo Tradition

The Stranger in the Cup – How to Read Your Luck and Fate in the
Tea Leaves by Gregory Lee White and Catherine Yronwode

How to Use Amulets, Charms, and Talismans in the Hoodoo and Conjure Tradition
by Catherine Yronwode and Gregory Lee White

Lenormand Basics – How to Read Lenormand Cards for Beginners

Casting Love Spells – Rituals of Romance, Passion, and Attraction

Hex Appeal – How to Cast Dark Spells of Revenge, Cursing, and Damnation

Fairy Lore and Myths

Papa Gee's Book of Candle Magic

Cernunnos – The Lord of Wild Things

INTRODUCTION

This is a book for those of us who have stood at a crossroads and felt the world go quiet. For those who've felt the pull of something older, deeper, and stranger calling to them when they look at the moon or light a flame. It's for anyone who has whispered a name in the dark and hoped someone was listening.
Hecate is many things: goddess, witch, torchbearer, protector, truth-teller, and fierce friend. She is the one who says, "You are not alone," when the road is uncertain. She walks with witches and outcasts, with those who speak to the dead and those who speak to themselves in the mirror trying to remember who they are.

What follows is not a rulebook. It is a map of sorts, drawn with ink, tears, dreams, and firelight. It is a guide for building a relationship with Hecate that is real and alive, not just studied or recited. I've included myths and history, rituals and reflections, because she speaks through all of it—but most of all, she speaks through *you*.

If you are holding this book, it means some part of you is ready. Ready to listen. Ready to remember. Ready to stand at the edge of the known and step into something sacred.

And if that's true, then you've already met her.

She is waiting. She is watching. She is holding the key. Now let's begin.
!

DEDICATION

To my friend, Virginia Tabor,
whose conversations continue to breathe life into the
names of the old Gods and Goddesses.

ACKNOWLEDGEMENTS

Love and thanks to everyone who, through their
enthusiasm on the topic, encouraged me to begin writing
a series of books about deities, gods, and goddesses.

THE HISTORY OF HECATE

Hecate is old—older than the Olympians, older than most of the gods people usually talk about. She comes from a time when the world still felt wild and sacred, when magic and mystery were part of daily life. Her story begins not in grand temples but in dark caves, at quiet crossroads, and beneath the night sky. She has always been a goddess of the edges.

In Greek myth, she is the daughter of Perses and Asteria. Her father's name means destruction, but not in a bad way—more like power that shakes the world. Her mother, Asteria, is the goddess of stars and nighttime prophecy. Together, they give Hecate the traits that define her: strength, mystery, vision, and magic.

Asteria's story is important. When Zeus pursued her, she refused to be taken. She turned into a quail and dove into the sea, becoming the island of Delos. This act of transformation, escape, and self-claiming echoes in Hecate's own nature. She is the goddess of change, the one who doesn't just adapt but *becomes* something new.

Unlike many ancient deities, Hecate wasn't limited to one place or city. People across the Greek world worshipped her. But they didn't build big temples in her name. Instead, they left offerings at the edges of towns, near gates, in caves, and especially at crossroads. These places were sacred to her—not because they were flashy, but because they were powerful. Crossroads are where decisions are made, where past and future meet, where one life ends and another begins.

In her earliest worship, Hecate was seen as a guardian of thresholds—not just physical doors and paths, but the unseen places between life and death, fear and courage, ignorance and truth. People left offerings at crossroads hoping she would protect them from harm or help them find the right direction. These weren't huge ceremonies, but quiet acts of devotion. Bread. Garlic. Eggs. Wine. Honey cakes. And always, the ritual was done in silence. Always, the offering was left behind without turning back.

She appears in many stories, but one of the most important is the tale of Persephone. When Persephone was taken into the Underworld, Hecate was the only one who heard her cries. She stood beside Demeter during her search and later became Persephone's guide as she traveled between worlds. In this myth, Hecate is not just a witness—she is a helper, a guide, and a bridge between the living and the dead.

She shows up again in the story of Medea, a witch who called on Hecate for help with her magic. Medea wasn't a sweet or simple character—she was powerful, dangerous, and deeply connected to the kind of magic that transforms everything it touches. The fact that she called on Hecate says a lot about how ancient people viewed the goddess: she was the one you called when you wanted real power.
Even as the gods of Olympus gained popularity, Hecate remained respected. In Hesiod's *Theogony*, Zeus himself honors her and gives her a share in all

things—earth, sea, and sky. This kind of respect from the king of the gods was rare. It means Hecate held a unique position, both within and beyond the usual divine structure. She wasn't just another goddess. She was something else.

Over time, her image evolved. She began to appear with three faces—sometimes three bodies—looking in different directions. She held torches, keys, daggers, and sometimes snakes. These weren't just symbols. They were tools. The torches lit the way. The keys opened doors between worlds. The dagger cut away illusion. The snake reminded us of rebirth, wisdom, and life beneath the surface.

She was honored during the Eleusinian Mysteries, an ancient set of secret rituals tied to death, rebirth, and the afterlife. Though little is known about these rites, we know that Hecate had a role in guiding people through them. Her presence helped initiates move through the shadows and come out transformed.

When the Roman Empire absorbed Greek culture, Hecate became known as Trivia. She was still the goddess of crossroads, still honored in the night, and still feared and respected. People placed statues of her at intersections to protect travelers. Her image was often three-headed—sometimes as a dog, a horse, and a lion—watching all directions at once.

Even after Christianity began to spread and the old gods were demonized, Hecate's name didn't disappear. In medieval Europe, witches still called on her. Some grimoires listed her as a demon, but others saw her as a source of power, wisdom, and insight.

She became a symbol of forbidden knowledge, of the things the world tried to bury but couldn't.

Today, Hecate has returned—not as a scary figure, but as a guide for those who seek truth, change, and personal power. Witches, Pagans, and spiritual seekers turn to her when they need to find their path, let go of the past, or protect what matters most. She is honored at the dark moon, at thresholds, and during moments of change.

She is a goddess of torches and keys. Of silence and speech. Of the dead and the living. Of endings and beginnings. She is the reason we don't fear the dark— we walk through it.

Hecate Statue, 3rd century AD, Turkey

RELICS AND SYMBOLS

Hecate is not just remembered in myths or prayers. She is honored through objects—things that carry her energy, her power, and her story. These sacred items are not just decorations. They are bridges between the world we see and the world we feel. Her symbols speak for her when there are no words. They protect. They guide. They remind us we are never alone.

Let's start with one of the most well-known symbols of Hecate: the triple-form statue, often called a Hecateion. This is a statue or carving of Hecate with three faces or three bodies joined together, usually facing in different directions. It represents her ability to see in all directions at once—past, present, and future. It also stands for her connection to the three worlds: the heavens, the earth, and the underworld. These statues were often placed at crossroads, doorways, and other threshold spaces to guard the people who passed by.

Each face on a Hekataion can also reflect her different forms: the maiden, the mother, and the crone. These three aspects of her help us understand that Hecate is with us through all stages of life. She doesn't belong to just one time. She belongs to every time.

In many of these statues, you'll also notice that she's holding tools: torches, keys, knives, or snakes. These are not just for show. They are part of her magic. Her torches light the path through the dark. Her keys open doors—sometimes real, sometimes spiritual. The dagger cuts away lies, illusions, or things that no longer serve. And the snake? The snake is a sign of rebirth, transformation, and ancient wisdom. Hecate holds the snake because she knows that to grow, we sometimes have to shed.

Another important symbol is the Hecate Wheel. This is a circular design with a spiral or maze-like shape inside. It stands for cycles—life, death, rebirth—and the connection between all things. When people use this symbol in their rituals, they might trace the lines with their finger while praying or meditating. It helps center the mind and bring clarity. It also reminds us that no matter where we are in our journey, we are still on the path.

People who worship Hecate also work with amulets, charms, and plaques that carry her image or symbols. These items were made in ancient times out of bronze, silver, or gold. They might show her holding her torch or standing with dogs by her side. Some have prayers or names carved into them. These amulets were often worn for protection or kept in homes and sacred spaces to invite Hecate's presence.

Offerings were another key part of working with Hecate. These weren't always grand or expensive. In fact, some of the most common offerings were foods like garlic, eggs, fish, bread, honey cakes, and wine. These were left at crossroads, doorways, or on home altars to thank her, to ask for her help, or to keep spirits at peace. This act was known as Hecate's Supper. People made these offerings during the dark moon, a time for cleansing, reflection, and renewal.

Ritual tools were also used to connect with Hecate. Bowls and chalices held wine or water for her. Daggers, sometimes inscribed with her name or symbols, were used to draw protective circles or to cut away unwanted energy. Every item had purpose. Every item told a story.

Hecate is often shown holding three tools: a torch, a key, and a dagger. The torch lights the unknown. The key opens what is hidden. The dagger protects and reveals. Together, these tools show the balance of her power. She brings light, she brings truth, and she brings strength.

She is also deeply connected to animals—especially black dogs. In ancient times, people believed that when dogs howled at night, it was because Hecate was near. Black dogs were seen as her guardians. Some were even sacrificed to her, though this is not a practice followed today. Instead, many modern witches honor her by working with the spirit of the dog as a symbol of loyalty and protection.

Other animals sacred to her include snakes, owls, and frogs. Snakes represent transformation and ancient wisdom. Owls are symbols of clear sight in darkness. Frogs, often found near water and thresholds, represent change and rebirth. These creatures are not just symbols—they are allies.

Hecate is also tied to certain trees, especially yew and cypress. These trees are often found in graveyards and are associated with death and transformation. Yew trees live a long time and can regrow from their own roots, showing the cycle of life and death. Cypress trees are seen as protectors of the dead. Using their wood or leaves in rituals can connect you to Hecate's energy.

There's another powerful symbol connected to her called the triple cross or triskelion. This shape, made of three spirals or lines branching from a center, reflects her triple nature and the three realms she rules. It also speaks of motion, progress, and eternal cycles.

Knot magic is one more way that people have honored her. Tying knots into cords or strings while speaking prayers or wishes can help bind or release energy. These knots become spells. They can carry protection, healing, or strength. When we work with knots, we weave our will into the world—and Hecate is there, guiding our hands.

All of these symbols and objects—the statues, the keys, the wheels, the offerings—show us something important. They remind us that magic is both sacred and simple. That you don't need fancy words or expensive tools to honor her. You just need intention, respect, and a heart that is open to change.

So next time you see a key, a black dog, or a fork in the road, pause. Think of Hecate. Maybe leave her a small offering. Maybe say a quick prayer. Maybe just whisper her name.

Because in that moment, you are not alone. You are in her presence.

Hecate with her dogs

PRAYER TO HECATE, KEEPER OF CROSSROADS

O Hecate, Torchbearer,
Guardian of the threshold and guide of the lost—
I call to You, She who walks between worlds,
Queen of the Night and Mistress of the Moon.
You who know the secret paths,
You who see what lies ahead,
Walk beside me now.

Great Lady of the Threefold Form,
You who stand where all roads meet—
Bless me with your sight.
Shine your light upon the path I fear to tread.
Unlock the doors that time has closed.
Show me the truth, no matter how dark,
And give me the strength to face it.

Keeper of keys, Holder of mysteries,
Witch Mother,
Teach me to trust my own power.
Let your hounds circle close and guard my steps.
Let no harm pass through your gates without my knowing.
Where curses linger, break them.
Where fear binds, free me.
Where shadow hides, bring wisdom—not dread.

I come to You not as master, But as seeker.
I bring no empty words,
Only the promise to walk in truth,
To listen when You speak,
And to honor the crossroads You place before me.

O Hecate,
In your flame, may I find clarity.
In your silence, may I learn discernment.
In your presence, may I stand whole.
So mote it be.

HECATE AT THE CROSSROADS

Crossroads have always been seen as places of mystery and magic. In ancient cultures, they were thought to be doorways between this world and the spirit world—a place where the living and the dead might cross paths. For witches and magical practitioners, the crossroads are sacred, and Hecate, goddess of the liminal, is their guardian and queen.

Hecate is the goddess of thresholds and turning points. She does not dwell in the comfort of what is known. Instead, she waits where paths meet, where choices must be made, and where uncertainty reigns. She is there when we stand between fear and action, between the old self and the new.

In ancient Greece, people honored Hecate by leaving offerings at three-way crossroads. These were known as Hecate's Suppers. Offerings usually included garlic, eggs, fish, bread, cakes, or wine. These items were carefully prepared and brought in silence, then left at the crossroad during the dark moon. It was important not to speak and never to look back—looking back invited wandering spirits to follow you home. The supper was not just for Hecate, but for the ghosts and spirits that traveled with her.

Even today, these rites continue. Many modern witches perform their own version of the Deipnon, cleaning their homes beforehand to clear out negative energy. They gather food or symbolic items and take them to a quiet crossroads—rural or urban—where they leave their offering in Hecate's name. Some light a candle or burn incense. Others simply bow their head and whisper a prayer. Always, there is a deep respect for the spirits of the place.

But Hecate's crossroads are more than physical places. They are spiritual crossroads, emotional ones, times in life when we must choose. Do I end this relationship? Do I move to a new place? Do I follow the path of magic? Hecate stands with us in these moments. She does not force us down one path or another, but she holds up the torch and says, "Look closely. Choose with courage."

When working magic at a crossroads, the space itself becomes the ritual. There is no need for a grand altar or fancy tools. The crossroads already holds ancient power. Here are several ways to work with Hecate at the crossroads:

THE CROSSROADS OFFERING RITUAL

This is a basic but powerful way to honor Hecate. On the night of the dark moon, prepare a small meal: bread, cheese, garlic, hard-boiled egg, or a small piece of cooked fish. Place the food in a biodegradable container or on a plate you plan to leave behind. Walk to the crossroads in silence. Leave the offering at the center or to the side—depending on what feels right to you. Say:

"Hecate of the Crossroads, Keeper of Keys, I offer you this meal with love and respect. Guide me through the unknown, Light the path that is mine to walk."

Leave in silence. Do not turn back.

PETITIONING FOR GUIDANCE

Sometimes we need help making a decision. Write your question on a small piece of paper and bring it with you. You may also carry a black candle, a sprig of mugwort or lavender, or a key. At the crossroads, hold your question in your hands. Speak it aloud or silently in your mind. Then bury the paper in the dirt or tear it into small pieces and scatter them. Say:

"Hecate, wise and watching, Show me the path I need to see. Help me choose with strength and heart."

Wait. You might feel a breeze, hear a distant sound, or feel a shift in your chest. These are signs. Her answer may come later—in dreams, through signs, or in a sudden knowing.

THE RITUAL OF RELEASE

Crossroads are not just for choosing—they are for letting go. To release something—a bad habit, fear, anger, or heartbreak—write it down. Bring it to the crossroads with a black candle or stone. Light the candle if safe to do so. Say:

"Hecate, Keeper of Thresholds, Take this burden from my hands. I leave it here to be transformed."

Burn the paper or bury it. Leave the candle behind or extinguish it with thanks. Walk away lighter.

CALLING THE SPIRITS

Hecate is known to walk with spirits, especially those who are lost or wandering. If you work with ancestors or spirits, the crossroads can be a place to invite them in. Bring photos, heirlooms, or offerings. Set them up in a temporary shrine. Light a candle. Speak their names. Ask Hecate to open the way:

"Torchbearer, Keyholder, Open the gates between worlds. Let the spirits who love me draw near."

Listen. Feel. Be respectful. When finished, close the space with words of gratitude. Always leave a portion of food for the spirits.

CROSSROADS DEVOTIONAL WALK

You don't always have to do something formal. Sometimes walking to the crossroads is enough. Choose a night when the moon is dark. Walk in silence. Bring your thoughts, your feelings, your hopes. When you arrive, sit. Breathe. Listen. Whisper a prayer:

"Lady of the Crossroads, You see what I cannot. I trust your sight, your silence, your shadow. Stay with me."

You may feel nothing, or you may feel a sudden sense of peace, strength, or awareness. This is her gift.

Some witches build small crossroads inside their homes. They use chalk to draw a cross on the floor, or they lay sticks, bones, or cords in the pattern of crossing paths. In the center, they place an offering: a candle, a key, or a piece of bread. This becomes a sacred space—one that Hecate recognizes. Here, they meditate, pray, or cast spells of decision and direction.

For those who cannot visit a physical crossroads, a crossroads visualization is a powerful substitute. Close your eyes and imagine standing at the meeting of four paths. Imagine Hecate standing nearby, holding her torches. See her offer you a key. What path calls to you? What are you ready to leave behind?

Remember: Hecate does not demand perfection. She asks only for honesty, courage, and respect. She is not a goddess of easy answers, but of clarity. She will not walk the path for you, but she will stand beside you while you do.

The crossroads are sacred because they are uncomfortable. They force us to pause. They show us that nothing stays the same. And that is why Hecate waits there—not to confuse us, but to empower us.

So when you find yourself unsure, afraid, or standing

between two lives—call her. Leave her a supper. Light a flame. Whisper her name. Then walk forward.

Because that, too, is her magic.

Hecate at the Crossroads

HECATE AND WITCHCRAFT

Hecate is the goddess most often called upon by witches—and for good reason. She is not just connected to magic. She is magic. She is the force that helps us change, grow, and transform. Witches across time have honored her as their queen, teacher, and guide. Whether casting spells, reading omens, or working with spirits, Hecate is never far from the scene.

In ancient Greece, powerful women like Medea and Circe were said to call upon Hecate when performing their spells. These myths show Hecate as a goddess of herbs, potions, and deep magical knowledge. She understands what most others cannot see. That is what makes her so important to the craft.

Today, modern witches work with Hecate in many different ways. Some follow traditional rituals passed down through books and oral history. Others create their own paths, based on dreams, signs, and what feels right. There is no one way to honor her. What matters most is sincerity and respect.

Working With Hecate in Your Craft

If you consider yourself a witch—whether beginner or experienced—Hecate can help you grow in your practice by guiding you through transformation, challenge, and spiritual awakening. As a liminal goddess who dwells at the thresholds of life and death, light and darkness, knowledge and mystery, Hecate teaches us to embrace both the seen and unseen. She rules over witchcraft, divination, herbal knowledge, necromancy, and the deeper mysteries of initiation. Whether you're learning to cast your first circle or refining years of magical work, Hecate meets you where you are—but she rarely leaves you where she found you. Her lessons often come through dreams, signs, and moments of sharp truth. If you are serious about growing, she will demand clarity, courage, and accountability.

There are many ways to invite her into your work. Begin by setting a space of respect—light a candle at a crossroads, offer garlic or eggs, or simply speak her name with intention. Hecate responds to sincerity more than ceremony.

CASTING A CIRCLE IN HER NAME

When you begin a spell or ritual, you may want to cast a circle to protect the space. You can call on Hecate to stand at the edge, guarding your work. You might say:

"Hecate, guardian of the veil, Stand at this circle's edge. Keep me safe in my working. Light the path of my spell."

Light a black or red candle at each corner of the circle. Imagine her dogs pacing just beyond the lines, watching and protecting you. You might also choose to light a candle and place it in the center of the circle devoted specifically to her or to represent the situation you are calling on her for.

INVOKE HER BEFORE A SPELL

Hecate's energy can strengthen your spellwork. Before casting a spell for protection, insight, or transformation, you can invite her into your space. Here's a simple invocation:

"Torchbearer, Keykeeper, Come into this space. Guide my hands, shape my words, Empower this spell."

Hold a key or candle as you speak. Let your body feel her strength. Then begin your work.

SPELLWORK FOR PROTECTION

One of Hecate's best-known roles is as protector— especially of women, outcasts, and travelers. If you feel unsafe or need extra strength, you can create a protection spell using her symbols.

You will need:

- A black candle
- A key or drawing of a key
- Salt or crushed garlic

Draw a circle with salt. Place the key and candle in the center. Light the candle and say: "Hecate, shield me from harm. Stand at my door. Let no evil cross my path. With your torch and hounds, protect me."

Let the candle burn safely or snuff it out and keep the key on you as a charm.

DIVINATION WITH HER HELP

Hecate is a goddess of prophecy and hidden knowledge. If you do tarot, use runes, or scry (gazing into water or mirrors), ask her to help you see clearly. Before you begin, place a key or picture of a black dog beside your tools. Light incense—like mugwort or myrrh—and say:

"Mistress of the veil, Open my eyes. Let truth rise from shadow. Let what is hidden be shown."

Then begin your reading. Don't rush. Trust what you feel.

HERBAL MAGIC AND HECATE

Hecate is linked with herbs, especially those that grow in the dark or near graveyards. Common herbs associated with her include:

- Yew
- Cypress
- Mugwort
- Garlic
- Mandrake

These can be burned as incense, placed in charm bags, or used in protection spells. Be cautious with poisonous plants—never handle or use herbs unless you know they are safe. There are countless books on magical herbalism for you to consult but when it comes to plants you don't know, always research.

SHADOW WORK WITH HECATE

Hecate is not afraid of darkness. She walks through fear, grief, and rage without flinching. If you are working on healing trauma, letting go of guilt, or facing hard truths, Hecate can help.

Create a safe, quiet space. Light a single candle. Hold a mirror or close your eyes. Say: "Lady of the dark moon, Help me see what I've hidden. Help me hold it with grace. Help me heal."

Breathe slowly. Let emotions rise. Write what comes to you. This is deep magic. Be gentle with yourself.

AN ALTAR TO HECATE

Having a space just for her is a powerful way to grow your connection. On your altar, you might place:

- A small statue or picture of her
- A black, red, or silver candle
- A key
- Garlic, eggs, or wine
- A figure of a dog, owl, or serpent

You can sit there in meditation, pray, or just be still. Speak to her like a wise friend. Ask her for guidance.

DAILY DEVOTION

You don't need to wait for the dark moon to honor Hecate. Here are small ways to bring her into your daily life:

- Light a candle in her name in the evening.
- Say a quick prayer before leaving the house.
- Whisper thanks when you find clarity.
- Leave small offerings at natural crossroads or in the woods.

Even a simple gesture—like drawing a key on your wrist—can remind you of her presence.

Hecate is not a goddess of fear. She is a goddess of strength. She is the one who walks beside you when the road is uncertain. She teaches you to trust your power, to use your voice, and to face the unknown with courage.

Whether you call her with a formal spell or a quiet whisper, she hears. She sees. And she answers— always in her own way.

To walk with Hecate is to walk a path of deep magic and self-truth. And if you're reading this now, maybe she's already calling you.

HECATE IN POP CULTURE

Hecate may come from the ancient world, but she's never truly disappeared. Her name and story have shown up in plays, books, TV shows, cartoons, and movies. Some of these stories show her in ways that match who she really is—a wise, powerful goddess of magic, crossroads, and transformation. Other times, people get her wrong, turning her into something scary or evil. But even when she's misunderstood, Hecate still stands out. People feel something when they hear her name. Her power leaves a mark.

One of the first famous times Hecate appeared in art was in the play *Macbeth* by William Shakespeare. In the story, she is shown as the queen of witches. She's angry that the other witches have done magic without asking her. She talks about chaos and danger, and she seems like someone who wants to be in control. This version of Hecate isn't very kind or wise, but it still made a big impact. For many years, people linked her name to mystery, magic, and fear because of this play. Even if it wasn't true to who she really is, it helped keep her name alive.

More recently, Hecate has been mentioned in several TV shows that deal with magic and the supernatural. In *Buffy the Vampire Slayer*, her name is used in spells. One spell calls on her to turn a person into a rat. It's a funny moment in the show, but it still connects her to the idea of transformation. That's a big part of who Hecate is—she helps people change, even when it's hard.

In *American Horror Story: Coven*, Hecate is mentioned as a protector of witches. She's not shown as a full character, but people in the story speak about her with respect and fear. Her name is used during rituals, and you can feel her presence, even if you don't see her. That's very true to how many modern witches experience her today. She doesn't always show up in loud or dramatic ways. Sometimes, you just *know* she's there—watching, guiding, and waiting for you to choose the right path.

Other shows don't always get it right. In the older TV show *Charmed*, there's an episode where Hecate is shown as a demon who wants to marry a human man and have a demon baby. This version has nothing to do with real myths or the goddess herself. It's made up for entertainment. But even so, it shows how her name still grabs people's attention. Writers and creators keep returning to her, even if they don't always understand her.

Books have done a better job of honoring Hecate's true spirit. In the *Percy Jackson* series by Rick Riordan, she shows up as a goddess of magic and crossroads. She's powerful, wise, and helps heroes who are facing hard choices. This matches how many witches see her today—as someone who doesn't make your choices for you, but who stands beside you when you're facing something important. She teaches responsibility and growth.

In *Practical Magic* by Alice Hoffman, Hecate isn't a main character, but she's part of the magical world in the background. The Owens family, who are witches, carry a quiet connection to her, as they demonstrate when they call upon her to bring Gillian's dangerous boyfriend back to life. That's how Hecate often shows up—quiet but strong, like a deep current beneath the surface. You don't always see her, but you know she's there.

She also appears in comic books, both in the DC and Marvel worlds. Sometimes she's shown as a goddess who once gave magic to the world but was punished for it. Other times, she's more mysterious, a powerful figure covered in shadows. These versions may not all match the real myths, but they keep her connected to themes of magic, mystery, and change. Whether she's seen as good or dangerous, Hecate is always tied to transformation.

Even cartoons have made space for her. In *Disney's Hercules: The Animated Series*, Hecate is shown as a magical goddess with a big personality and strong powers. It's a fun, kid-friendly version, but it still shows that her name and story are powerful enough to be part of modern tales—even in cartoons. That says a lot.

So why does Hecate keep showing up in so many different stories? Because she stands for something we all face: the moment of choice. She is the feeling we get when we're standing between two paths, unsure of what comes next. She is the magic in that moment. She reminds us that change is not something to fear—it's part of life. She helps us face our shadows and find our strength.

Even when her story is changed, or when people don't get her right, something true still comes through. Her name makes people stop and think. Writers, artists, witches, and seekers all feel her pull. She reminds us that the dark isn't empty—it's full of power and potential. And when we walk into that darkness, we don't walk alone. She's already there, holding the torch.

So the next time you hear her name in a book, movie, or show, take a closer look. What version of Hecate is being shown? What message is being shared? What parts of her story are still alive—and what parts have been forgotten? These questions matter. Because Hecate isn't just a symbol. She's a guide. And if you pay attention, she just might show you the way.

In the movie Practical Magic, the sisters call upon Hecate to help them bring back someone from the dead

WAYS TO WORK WITH HER

Hecate is not a goddess you visit once in a while. She is the kind of presence that grows with you. The more time you give her, the more she shows you. Working with Hecate isn't about memorizing spells or having the right tools—it's about building a relationship that lasts. She teaches slowly, through silence, through signs, and through moments when you feel like no one else is watching but her.

In this chapter, we'll go deep into ways you can connect with her—whether you're brand new to magic or have walked the path for years. These are living practices, full of soul and power. Take what calls to you. Leave what doesn't. Come back later. That's how it works with her.

CREATING SACRED SPACE

Your space doesn't need to be fancy. It just needs to be real. Whether it's a small shelf, a corner of your bedroom, or a table in the woods, make it yours. Clean it with care. Add what feels sacred. Here are just a few suggestions for things you might include:

- A black or red candle
- A small statue, print, or image of Hecate
- A bowl of water and a small dish of salt
- Keys, especially old ones
- Symbols of her animals: dog, snake, owl, or frog
- Herbs like garlic, mugwort, lavender, or yew

Once you have your altar or sacred spot, sit with it often. Light a candle. Speak out loud or silently. Ask questions. Leave offerings. This is how relationships are built—with time and presence.

SIMPLE PRACTICES OF DEVOTION

You don't have to do something big every day to honor Hecate. Magic is in the small things. Try these:

- Light a candle at dusk and say her name.
- Whisper a short prayer before you leave your house.
- Touch the key on your necklace and ask for protection.
- Keep a small stone or herb in your pocket as a reminder of her.
- Notice the moon and how it changes. Speak to it.

Daily devotion is about remembering her, noticing her, and making room for her in your thoughts and actions.

WORKING WITH THE MOON

Hecate is deeply tied to the moon—especially the dark moon, when the sky is black and quiet. This is a time to go inward, to let go, and to prepare for rebirth. Here are some ways to work with Hecate during the moon phases:

- **Dark Moon (New Moon Eve):** Offer food at a crossroads. Clean your home spiritually. Burn paper with what you want to release.

- **Waxing Moon:** Ask for help in beginning something new. Light white or silver candles. Write out your hopes.
- **Full Moon:** Celebrate her power. Do divination. Leave flowers or incense on her altar.
- **Waning Moon:** Focus on endings. Cut cords. Ask for strength to face truth.

You can create moon rituals with just a candle, your voice, and intention. Or you can go all out with herbs, incense, songs, and a full altar setup. Either way, she listens.

OFFERINGS AND GIFTS

Hecate is a goddess of generosity and exchange. Offerings are a way to show love, respect, and thanks. Some ideas:

- Garlic, eggs, bread, honey, or red wine
- Handmade items (charms, poems, paintings)
- Things from nature (stones, feathers, herbs)
- Acts of kindness in her name (helping animals, protecting the vulnerable)

When you leave an offering, speak from your heart and always when you are in the right frame of mind – never when you're rushed to do other things:

"Hecate, I give this with love. For what you have shown me, For the light you hold in dark times." Always be respectful. Never leave trash. Never offer what you wouldn't eat or use yourself.

Prayers and Invocations

Words are spells. They shape energy. You don't need fancy language to speak to Hecate. But if it helps, here are a few to try:

Morning Prayer

"Hecate, watch over my day. Guide my steps. Steady my spirit. Let me see clearly and walk with purpose."

Evening Prayer

"Lady of the Crossroads, I thank you. For the choices, for the signs, for the strength. Be with me through dreams and silence."

Call for Protection

"Hecate, hold the key. Guard the door. Keep harm away and peace within."

Write your own. Keep them in a notebook. Say them aloud or in your heart.

RITUALS FOR TRANSFORMATION

Hecate helps us change—not just small changes, but deep ones. Here's a powerful ritual you can do when you are ready to let go of an old part of yourself and call in the new. In some traditions, this might be considered a type of 'cut and clear' spell.

You will need:
- A black candle
- A mirror
- A small piece of paper and pen

Light the candle. Sit with the mirror. Look into your own eyes and speak: "I see who I've been. I honor them. But now I change. Now I grow. With Hecate as my guide, I cross the threshold." Write down what you are releasing. Burn or bury the paper. Blow out the candle. Sit in the dark for a moment. Then say: "I rise. I return. I begin again."

DREAM WORK AND SPIRIT MESSAGES

Hecate often comes through dreams. To invite her, try this before bed:

- Light a candle and say: "Hecate, come into my dreams. Show me what I need to see."
- Place a key or small offering near your pillow.
- Keep a journal by your bed. Write down anything that comes, even if it's confusing. Patterns will emerge.

You may also hear her through signs during the day. A black dog appears. A crossroads shows up in a dream. You keep seeing keys. Pay attention. Spirit speaks in symbols.

SEASONAL CELEBRATIONS

You can honor Hecate during the Wheel of the Year. Here are a few ideas:

- **Samhain (Oct 31–Nov 1):** Leave offerings for her and for your ancestors. Do shadow work.
- **Winter Solstice:** Light her torches. Ask for guidance through the darkness.
- **Spring Equinox:** Plant seeds—literal or magical—and ask for her blessing on growth.
- **August 13:** A day sacred to Hecate. Hold a vigil, offer garlic, and honor her protection of the land.

Let your seasonal practices be creative. Let them come from your heart.

WALKING WITH HER LONG-TERM

Working with Hecate is a journey. Some days you will feel her strongly. Other days you may not. That's okay. She is patient. She waits at the edge of your knowing. She meets you when you are ready.
Here are some signs she may be calling you:

- You feel drawn to keys, torches, or crossroads.
- You dream of dogs, snakes, or the moon.
- You are facing big changes or feel stuck between paths.
- You feel a quiet voice in the dark saying, "Trust yourself."

If this sounds like you, don't be afraid. Just begin. Light a candle. Speak her name. Leave her something small. And most of all—listen.

Hecate is not a goddess who shouts. She waits for silence. For courage. For honesty. And when you are ready, she comes to walk beside you—not as a master, but as a guide.

She is the one who says: "You already hold the key. Let me show you the door."

IN MODERN PAGANISM

Hecate has found a place in the hearts of many modern Pagans, witches, and Wiccans—not as a distant memory, but as a living, powerful presence. She is honored, called upon, and deeply loved. Though ancient, her spirit speaks clearly to the needs of today. She shows up when we're in transition, when we're searching for strength, or when we need to trust our inner voice.

Across many Pagan paths, Hecate is seen as a goddess of transformation, magic, protection, and wisdom. Wiccans may call to her during rituals, full moons, or sabbats. Others may honor her through daily devotion, altar work, or spellcasting. However she is approached, one truth remains—Hecate's voice is still strong, and she listens.

WHY SHE SPEAKS TO US NOW

Many people find Hecate at a crossroads. That's no accident. She shows up when life is shifting—after a loss, at the start of a new journey, or during a deep awakening. She is the goddess of thresholds, of choices, of becoming.

In Wiccan belief, Hecate is often linked to the Crone—the wise, final face of the Triple Goddess. But she is more than that. Some see her as Maiden, Mother, and Crone all at once. She holds past, present, and future. She walks with the dead and lights the way for the living.

People turn to her because she helps us face our shadows. She reminds us that we always have a choice. She guards our homes, dreams, and spirits. And she supports real magic—the kind that changes you from the inside out.

HOW SHE IS HONORED

Wiccans may call on Hecate during moon rituals, especially Esbats, or at seasonal festivals called Sabbats. Some work with her regularly, while others seek her only in moments of need.

There are many ways to honor her. Lighting a candle and saying her name. Leaving offerings at a crossroads, on an altar, or in the wild. Creating rituals for growth and change. Doing shadow work, speaking with ancestors, or calling to spirits. Meditating with her symbols—keys, torches, the moon—also deepens the bond.

Some Wiccans choose Hecate as a matron goddess. That means she becomes their central guide and teacher. This relationship isn't built in a single ritual—it grows over time, through listening, trust, and steady practice.

THE DARK MOON AND HER MAGIC

The dark moon—when the moon disappears from the sky—is a powerful time to work with Hecate. It's a time of release, closure, and quiet strength. During the dark moon, witches and Wiccans may ask her for wisdom and protection. Some rituals are simple: a whisper, a candle, a quiet offering. Others are more formal—casting a circle, calling the elements, and doing deeper spellwork.

A prayer might sound like this:
Lady Hecate, I walk with you tonight,
Through the dark, through the stillness, through the truth.
Help me let go of what I no longer need.
Help me remember who I truly am.

These words are not just poetry—they are an opening, a reaching out. And Hecate listens.

SACRED SYMBOLS AND TOOLS

Those who walk with Hecate often surround themselves with her symbols. Keys represent hidden knowledge and the doors we choose to open. Torches light the way through darkness. Dogs, her faithful companions, stand for loyalty and spiritual protection. The moon—especially when waning or dark—reflects her mystery and power. And crossroads, real or imagined, are sacred to her as places of decision and transformation.

Altars may include candles, incense, stones, herbs, or personal objects that feel connected to her. Some people dedicate part of their home or garden to Hecate—a place for prayer, silence, or ritual. What matters most is intention.

CELEBRATION

Hecate can be honored alone or as part of a Wiccan sabbat. As I already mentioned, certain days are especially powerful. Samhain, on October 31st, is a time when many call on her for guidance with ancestors or the spirit world. At the Winter Solstice, she may be honored as the light that leads us through the cold dark. Beside August, February 16th is known in some traditions as Hecate's Night—a time for candle rituals and deep reflection. August 13th is an older day of observance, when she is remembered as a protector of land and city.

These celebrations don't have to be elaborate. Lighting a candle, sharing a meal, making a spell jar, or simply sitting in nature with an open heart—these all count as acts of devotion.

HECATE'S PLACE IN MODERN TRADITIONS

Some entire magical paths are built around Hecate's worship. In Hellenic Reconstructionism, practitioners try to honor her in ways similar to ancient Greece. Others are more modern and fluid, such as the Temple of Hekate—a loose network of devotees with different practices but the same love for the goddess. Devotional witchcraft is another path, where a person builds their magical life around a central deity like Hecate.

Thanks to books, social media, and a rising interest in witchcraft, many are finding her for the first time. And they're realizing something powerful: Hecate speaks to all kinds of people. The healer and the rebel. The dreamer and the realist. The young beginner and the seasoned elder. She comes to different people at unique times in their life when she is needed.

SHADOW WORK AND SELF-DISCOVERY

Shadow work is common in modern Pagan practice. It means facing the parts of ourselves we usually avoid—our anger, grief, fear, or shame. It's hard work. But it's sacred.

Hecate is one of the few goddesses who walks with us into those hidden places. She does not turn away. She does not scold. She simply says, *"This is part of you. Now let's see what it can become."*

Shadow work might look like journaling during the dark moon, meditating with a candle and mirror, asking her for clarity, or exploring old dreams and childhood wounds. It's not about perfection. It's about honesty. And healing.

A LIVING PRESENCE

Hecate is not just a figure from the past. She is alive in the present. She walks city streets and forest trails. She shows up in rituals and quiet thoughts. She watches over our doorways—both the ones we close, and the ones we dare to open.

For Wiccans and Pagans, she is a guide through life's thresholds. She helps us honor our inner voice, face what's real, and step into our own power. Whether you're in a coven or walking alone, whether you follow Greek gods or a mixed path, Hecate has wisdom to offer.

She is the torch in the dark. The whisper in silence. The steady hand at your back when you're afraid to move forward.

And she is always ready to walk beside you—if you light the candle and call her name.

The Hecate Chiaramonti a Roman sculpture of triple-bodied Hecate after a Hellenistic original

HECATE'S ROLE IN ASTROLOGY & DIVINATION

Hecate isn't just a goddess of crossroads and torches. She also watches the stars, whispers through the moon, and speaks through cards and runes. Her energy flows through astrology and divination like a deep river of knowing. If you've ever felt drawn to the mysteries of fate, the pull of the moon, or the power of a tarot reading, then you've already stepped into her realm.

HECATE AND THE NIGHT SKY

The stars have always been used to track time, predict events, and understand personality. Astrology is the language of the sky. Hecate, as a goddess of magic and mystery, is linked to many of the symbols and planets used in astrological charts.

One of the most direct connections is the asteroid Hekate, numbered 100 in the catalog of asteroids. It is found in the main belt between Mars and Jupiter. It's not one of the planets, but it can still show up in your birth chart and tell a story about how Hecate's energy plays out in your life. When astrologers look at where Hekate sits in a chart, they consider questions like:

- Where do you face turning points?
- Where are you called to choose between paths?
- Where do you hold hidden wisdom or fear?

THE ASTEROID HECATE IN YOUR CHART

To find Hekate in your chart, you can use online astrology tools that let you add asteroids. Once you find her, note the zodiac sign and the house she's in. These give clues to her influence.

- If Hekate is in the 1st house, you may feel her in your identity and how you meet the world.
- In the 4th house, her energy could be tied to your ancestors, home life, or emotional foundation.
- In the 8th house, she may show up in deep transformation, magic, or connection with the dead.

Her sign placement colors her energy. Hekate in Aries might make you a bold magical pioneer. In Scorpio, she may call you to work in the shadows, healing pain and uncovering truth.

HECATE, THE MOON, THE DARK PHASE

In astrology, the moon represents emotions, intuition, and cycles. Hecate is especially connected to the moon's darker phases—the waning and dark moon. This is the time to:

- Reflect
- Release
- Rest
- Renew

If you were born during a dark moon, you may naturally carry Hecate's energy—quiet, deep, wise, and able to see what others avoid. You may also feel drawn to work with her around the new moon or during lunar eclipses.

Hecate's energy also shows up when the moon makes connections to Pluto (the planet of death and rebirth), Saturn (the keeper of time and boundaries), and Neptune (the dreamer, the mystic). Watch for these in your own chart or when doing moon rituals.

DIVINATION AND HECATE

Divination is a way of listening—of asking the unseen for insight. Hecate has always been linked to prophecy and oracles. In ancient times, her priests and priestesses gave messages through trance, dreams, and signs. You can still call on her today through tools like:

- Tarot
- Runes
- Pendulums
- Scrying mirrors
- Dreams
- Tea leaf reading

When using these tools, you might:

- Light a black or purple candle
- Say a simple invocation like: "Hecate, seer of shadow, Walk with me. Help me see what is true."
- Place her symbols nearby—keys, bones, herbs, or a photo
- Keep a journal of what you hear, see, or feel

TAROT AND HECATE

Some tarot cards feel especially linked to Hecate:

- **The High Priestess:** Keeper of mysteries, symbol of hidden truth.
- **Death:** Not about ending, but transformation—her favorite thing.
- **The Moon:** Shadows, dreams, illusions, and deep intuition.
- **The Hermit:** Holding a lamp, lighting the way—just like her torches.

If these cards show up often, it may be a sign that Hecate is near or that her energy is guiding your current path.

RUNE MAGIC AND SIGNS

Runes are ancient symbols used for writing, magic, and divination. Some that may carry Hecate's energy include:

- **Perthro:** The unknown, fate, hidden forces
- **Hagalaz:** Storms, breaking patterns, deep change
- **Eiwaz:** Connection to the dead, trees, and the unseen world

When casting runes, let your hands rest over them and ask: "Hecate, speak through the runes. What do I need to know?"

Take your time. Let the meanings rise like smoke. Her answers are often quiet but clear.

DREAM WORK AND PROPHECY

Hecate speaks through dreams. She might appear as a woman in shadow, a dog, a torch, or even a path that splits in two. To invite her:

- Place a bowl of water and a key near your bed
- Burn mugwort incense or place a bit under your pillow (in a safe pouch)
- Say before sleep: "Hecate, show me what I must know. Let the dream be your torch."

Record what you see. Over time, patterns will form.

CREATE A DIVINATION RITUAL

You can build a full ritual around divination. Here's a basic outline:

1. **Cleanse the space** – Burn incense or sprinkle saltwater.
2. **Light a candle** – Black, purple, or dark blue.
3. **Place her symbols** – Keys, bones, herbs, or art.
4. **Call on her** – Speak from your heart or use a written prayer.
5. **Use your tool** – Pull tarot cards, cast runes, gaze into water.
6. **Close the space** – Thank her. Blow out the candle. Record what you learned.

Astrology and divination are about trust. Trust in the signs. Trust in your intuition. Trust that the answers will come—even if they arrive slowly.

Hecate doesn't shout. She whispers. She shows you one step at a time. But when you honor her, and truly listen, she gives insight that goes beyond the surface. She reminds you of your power. She reveals the path you didn't know was there.

With her as your guide, you don't need to fear the unknown. You were made to walk through it.

It is common practice to cast a circle before performing magical rituals

HECATE AND THE ANCESTORS

Hecate is a goddess of deep roots. She is a guide through the shadowed places, a watcher of thresholds, and a companion to the dead. When we call on her to help us connect with our ancestors, she hears us. And if we listen, she will show us how to honor what has come before—so we can live more fully in the present.

In the ancient world, Hecate stood close to the dead. People honored her at the edges—of towns, of roads, of graves. She ruled those in-between places where spirits pass and linger. Offerings were left not just for her, but for the souls who followed in her wake. She wasn't feared as a captor of the dead, but respected as their guide. She carried a torch through the darkness. She made the path safe.

Today, many witches and Pagans still turn to Hecate in their ancestor work. Whether you are honoring blood relatives, chosen family, spiritual teachers, or cultural ancestors, Hecate opens the door between this world and the next. She stands with you at the altar. She listens when you speak their names. And sometimes, if the spirits are willing, she brings them close enough to answer.

WHY WE WORK WITH ANCESTORS

Each of us carries more than our own story. We carry the stories of those who came before us—their choices, their pain, their wisdom, and their prayers.

Some of it we inherited in our DNA. Some in the way we were raised. Some in silence, secrets, or dreams.

Working with ancestors helps us understand those patterns. It helps us find peace with the past and change the future. We can name old wounds so they don't rule us anymore. We can claim strength from those who loved fiercely, survived deeply, and kept going. When we do this work with Hecate's presence, it becomes sacred. She clears the way between the worlds so we can move forward with confidence and care.

CREATING AN ANCESTRAL ALTAR

If you want to begin ancestor work, start by making space for it. You don't need much. What matters is intention and respect.

Choose a small table or shelf. Lay down a dark cloth—black, deep red, or dark gray. Place photos, heirlooms, or written names of your ancestors. Add a candle (black, white, or red), a bowl of water to welcome spirit presence, and something that represents Hecate—a key, a torch, or a small statue. Offerings can be as simple as bread, honey, wine, or fruit.

Light the candle and say:

"Hecate, Keeper of Spirits,
Stand at this altar with me.
Open the path so I may honor those who came before."

Speak the names of your ancestors. Say what you remember. Or just sit quietly and let your heart open. You may feel warmth, a sudden emotion, or the air shift around you. These are signs. Someone is listening.

SPEAKING WITH THE DEAD

You do not need to be a psychic to speak to your ancestors. You only need to listen with care and show up with honesty.

When you're ready, cast a simple circle or say a protection prayer. Light incense—something sacred to you, like myrrh, mugwort, or lavender. Place your hands on the altar and say:

"Spirits of my blood, my people, my line—
I call to you in peace.
Come close, if you will."

You can speak a question aloud or write it down. Ask for guidance. Ask what needs to be healed. Then sit, breathe, and listen. Some use tarot cards, pendulums, or scrying tools to help translate what comes. Others rely on feeling. When you're done, thank them:

"Thank you for your presence
Thank you for showing up for me.
Thank you for your guidance.
I honor your memory."

Blow out the candle. Close your circle. And rest. This kind of work is powerful, even when it feels small.

Shadow Work and Family Healing

Some of what we inherit isn't light. Abuse. Addiction. Shame. Secrets. These shadows don't disappear on their own. But they can be faced. And with Hecate at your side, they can be transformed.

Try this practice when you're ready to release something that runs through your family line. Write down the pattern. Be clear—name it. Fold the paper and place it under a black stone on your altar. Say:

"Hecate, Witness of Wounds,
Help me see the truth in love.
Help me end what must not continue."

Repeat the prayer each day for seven days. On the last day, burn the paper or bury it in the earth. What we bury with respect does not haunt us. It teaches us, and then it lets us go.

Offerings and Holy Days

You don't need a feast to feed the spirits. Simple offerings speak loudest when they're given with heart. A glass of water. A slice of bread. A bit of wine or tobacco. Leave them on your altar and say:

"This is for those who came before.
May you be honored.
May you be at peace."

The most powerful time to work with Hecate and the ancestors is Samhain—October 31st. The veil is thin. Light candles in every window. Cook a meal your family would know. Set out a plate. Speak their names. Welcome them.

But you can honor them anytime. On their birthdays. On the day they passed. During the dark moon. Or whenever your spirit feels called. Hecate is present at every threshold.

When You Don't Know Your Ancestors
Not everyone has a clear picture of where they come from. Some were adopted. Some were disconnected from culture or kin. Some come from families full of pain. You can still do this work.

Call out to the ancestors who walk with kindness. Say:

"I call to my kindest ancestors.
Those who walk with love.
You are welcome here."

Hecate helps open the path for the ones who mean you well. Over time, you may dream of them. You may see signs, feel a presence, or hear a name whispered in your spirit. Don't rush it. Just keep showing up.

WALKING WITH HECATE

Hecate stands at the gate between the living and the dead. She is not a goddess of fear—she is a guardian of memory. A keeper of truth. When you come to her altar with love in your heart and courage in your hands, she will guide you. She will help you listen. And she will walk beside you as you make peace with the past.

Because in the end, we are never truly alone. The ones who came before walk with us still. And with Hecate's help, we can learn to hear their footsteps, feel their prayers, and carry their wisdom forward.

Let their stories become your strength. Let her torch light your path.

Hecate is often shown as three women standing back to back because she holds the power of the crossroads—where past, present, and future meet. This triple form reflects her role as a goddess of thresholds, change, and deep wisdom. She sees in all directions and moves through all stages of life: Maiden, Mother, and Crone

THE UNDERWORLD

To know Hecate is to know the shadows—not just the darkness of night, but the inner terrain of fear, silence, and change. She is not just a goddess of magic and thresholds. She is also a goddess of the Underworld. And she does not rule there with fear— but with firelight.

The Underworld is not only the realm of the dead. It is a place of transformation. A place where we are stripped down to our truth, our wounds, our essence. Hecate is the one who guides us there and, more importantly, the one who brings us back.

In the myth of Persephone, when the maiden goddess is taken to the Underworld by Hades, Hecate is the one who hears her cries. She becomes the companion of Demeter in the search. Later, she becomes the one who walks beside Persephone on her yearly journey in and out of the realm of the dead.

This is important. Hecate does not live in the Underworld—but she can go there. She moves between the worlds with ease. She is a psychopomp— a guide of souls. This makes her an essential goddess for those who do inner healing, grief work, or spirit contact.

The Underworld is more than a place beneath the earth. It is a state of being. Times of depression, deep grief, spiritual crisis, trauma recovery, or major transformation all mirror the mythic journey to the Underworld. When we feel lost, buried, or broken, we are in that realm. And Hecate is there, holding her torches, reminding us: this is not the end. This is the beginning of something new.

One way to connect with Hecate as a guide through the Underworld is through visualization. You can imagine yourself standing before a cave, holding a black candle. You take a breath, and Hecate appears, offering you her torch. You walk into the cave together. Inside, you may find memories, emotions, or truths you've buried. Trust that she is with you. When you are ready, she shows you the way back out.

A ritual for Underworld healing may involve a black candle, a mirror, and a small key. Light the candle. Sit before the mirror or a bowl of still water. Say aloud or silently:

"Hecate, Keeper of Thresholds, guide me through the dark. Help me see what must be seen. Help me return wiser."

Then sit with your reflection. Ask yourself what needs to be faced. What part of you is ready to be healed? Write it down. Cry if you need to. Breathe. When you're ready, snuff the candle and thank Hecate for her presence.

Her tools in this space are powerful. The torch becomes a light of truth, revealing what's been hidden. The key becomes a symbol of freedom—the way out you didn't see before. Many who go through dark times carry a key on their altar or wear one around their neck. It is a reminder: this is temporary. There is a way through.

Hecate's presence is also felt in death work and grief. She is often called upon by those who work with the dying or the spirits of the dead. If you've lost someone, you can light a candle in their honor and ask Hecate to guide them safely. Speak their name. Tell them what's in your heart. Trust that your words will be carried across the veil.

Some symbols that help ground this work include bones, stones, poppies, and the pomegranate. Bones remind us of mortality and the strength that remains. Poppies symbolize rest, peace, and dreams. The pomegranate, sacred to Persephone, is the fruit of life and death held together. These can be added to your altar or carried with you when doing heavy emotional work.

You might choose to create an Underworld altar. Drape it in dark cloth. Add a candle or torch symbol, a mirror, a bowl of water, bones, or keys. Sit before it when you're grieving or in transformation. Make it a place of safety and truth. A place where you don't have to hide from your own pain.

And always, always remember: Hecate doesn't promise you won't feel afraid. But she promises to walk beside you while you feel it. She stands at the door of every ending and every beginning. With her, the Underworld is not a trap. It is a rite of passage. Think of it as a beginning, not an end. Because that is how all beginnings begin – with an ending.

So if you find yourself in the dark, call her. Say her name. Hold a key in your hand. Trust that she is near.

Hecate fighting the Giant – Pergamon altar

Temple of Hecate in Lagina, Caria. Caria was an ancient region in southwestern Asia Minor, now part of Turkey.

HECATE IN FOLK MAGIC

Hecate's name is most often spoken in connection to ancient Greece, but her spirit—the essence of the torchbearer, the crossroads guardian, the witch's guide—has touched many magical traditions around the world. Wherever there is a doorway between the worlds, wherever witches whisper to the night, her shadow lingers.

In folk magic, spirits like Hecate often appear not just as named deities but as forces—raw, mysterious, and powerful. In some cases, she is called by a different name. In others, she is not named at all but felt in the rituals and rites that take place at crossroads, in graveyards, near thresholds, and at the edges of towns.

In Southern folk traditions like Hoodoo and conjure, the crossroads is a sacred space where deals are struck, spirits are called, and magic is born. Though Hecate is not named in these traditions, the work done at these intersections reflects her influence. The crossroads is not just a meeting place—it's a spirit portal, a magical ground for transformation, and a channel for petitioning unseen forces. In this way, Hecate shares kinship with African-derived spirits like Papa Legba or Eshu, who guard the gates between the mortal world and the divine.

In Slavic witchcraft, spirits of the dead and ancestral guides are honored at the liminal times—sunset, midnight, twilight. Offerings of bread, salt, and water are left at thresholds, windowsills, and cross-paths.

This mirrors Hecate's traditional offerings during the Deipnon, when her followers left food at doorways and intersections for both the goddess and the hungry dead who followed her.

In traditional Italian Stregoneria (witchcraft), women known as *streghe* worked with spirits of the land, ancestors, and the moon. While not always called Hecate, these spirits held many of the same traits: they were guardians of hidden knowledge, midwives of change, and protectors of the home. Some Italian witches today openly worship Hecate as a goddess of both Old World and New World magic—uniting her Greek roots with their cultural heritage.

Even in Celtic traditions, there are echoes of her power in goddesses like The Cailleach, a crone deity of storms, winter, and fate. Though separate figures, both Hecate and The Cailleach embody the fierce wisdom of old age and the magic of endings that lead to new beginnings.

In modern folk magic, Hecate is often woven into candle spells, herbal workings, and protective charms. Practitioners may light black candles for her during difficult times, speak to her before casting a hex or curse, or call on her to help break generational cycles. She is especially strong in uncrossing work—magic meant to lift spiritual blockages and cleanse harmful energy.

A simple folk spell to call on her protection might look like this:
At midnight on a dark moon, place a black candle in the window. Write your fear or trouble on a small

scrap of paper. Fold it three times and place it under the candle. Say:

"Hecate, Lady of Night, Take this weight, make it light. Crossroads queen, fierce and free, Watch and shield and walk with me."

Let the candle burn as long as you safely can. Then bury the paper at a crossroads, in a cemetery (with permission), or in a pot of soil at your door.

In urban areas, modern witches are creating new forms of folk magic that echo old ways. Apartment doorways become altars. Fire escapes are treated like sacred thresholds. Subway stations are their crossroads. These witches leave coins, bread, or notes written in lipstick as offerings to Hecate and the spirits of the city.

In Brazil and other parts of South America, you'll find devotion to Pomba Gira, a spirit of love, crossroads, and justice often honored at midnight with offerings of cigarettes, champagne, and red roses. While not Hecate, Pomba Gira holds many of the same qualities—she stands at the edge of society, protects women and outcasts, and teaches empowerment through fearless self-expression.

These global threads reveal something powerful: Hecate's energy does not belong to one culture alone. She belongs to the liminal. She belongs to those who walk between worlds. She is found wherever witches light candles, wherever ancestors are called, wherever magic is whispered with reverence and courage.

So whether you practice Hoodoo, Appalachian folk magic, Stregoneria, Wicca, or your own blend of traditions—Hecate can walk beside you. She speaks the language of the soul. She understands the herbs in your cupboard and the bones buried in your yard. She knows your grief and your strength.

Folk magic is the magic of survival. It's the magic of people who had to learn how to protect themselves, how to heal each other, how to speak to the spirits when no one else would listen. Hecate thrives in that kind of magic.

Devotees making offerings to Hecate

HECATE AND QUEER IDENTITY

Hecate has always been a goddess of the in-between—the crossroads, the thresholds, the spaces where old rules fall away. For many queer people, that liminal space is home. It is the place where identity is forged, where we learn to survive, transform, and reclaim power. This is why so many queer witches and magical practitioners feel drawn to her. She sees us. She walks with us. And she meets us exactly where we are.

In ancient stories, Hecate was never limited by a single form. She was maiden, mother, and crone all at once. She ruled over the heavens, the earth, and the underworld. She could be one woman or three. She held opposites in balance—life and death, light and dark, silence and song. For queer folks who have lived between expectations, between names, between bodies or pronouns or paths, Hecate offers a kind of radical acceptance. She doesn't demand clarity. She honors complexity.

Queerness, like Hecate herself, is liminal. It exists beyond the old borders. It asks, "What else is possible?" And Hecate, torch in hand, answers, "More than you were told."

In magical practice, many queer people find healing in calling on Hecate. She gives us permission to shape ourselves anew. She reminds us that we are allowed to hold many truths at once. For those who have been cast out by family, religion, or society, Hecate becomes chosen family. She becomes protector, witness, and fierce ally.

Some queer witches create altars just for her—a place to sit in their truth without the pressures of what society calls "normal.". On these altars, they may place symbols of transformation: snakes, keys, mirrors, scissors, bones. They may light candles to honor both the self they were and the self they are becoming. In the quiet, they speak to Hecate not as an outsider but as someone who understands the path of becoming.

Rituals with Hecate can be deeply personal. A transgender practitioner might ask her to bless a name change. Someone coming out later in life might invoke her during a dark moon for strength. A nonbinary witch might see her as the embodiment of fluid power—neither one thing nor the other, but all things in sacred balance.

Hecate doesn't just tolerate the queer experience. She magnifies it. She shows us that queerness is magic. That transition is ritual. That choosing your truth is a kind of spell. And when the world tries to shame or silence us, she stands beside us, whispering, "No one gets to tell you who you are."

In myth, Hecate was feared as a witch goddess, a keeper of ghosts and wild places. In society, queer people have also been feared, misunderstood, and pushed to the edges. But there's power on the edges. There's freedom. And Hecate reigns there.

If you feel like you've never quite fit in, that your truth doesn't match what others expect—know this: you are not broken. You are not lost. You are simply standing at a sacred crossroads. And Hecate is already there, torch lit, waiting for you to speak your name.

She is the goddess who honors all who walk with courage. She is the one who turns shame into power. She is the one who says, "You are enough."

A PRAYER TO HECATE FOR CALMING THE QUEER SOUL

Great Hecate,
Keeper of crossroads and all things betwixt and between,

I call to You from the edge of what is seen and what is known.
I stand in the name of all who have been called strange,
All who have been shamed, erased, or hidden.

I honor the blood of queer ancestors who walked alone,
Who loved in silence, who prayed in secret,
Who dared to be when the world told them not to be.

Hecate, You who hold the keys,
Unlock the doors that fear has sealed.
Break the chains of guilt, of false teachings, of internal war.
Let my heart be a temple where no part of me is cast out.

Make whole what has been divided.
Let Your dogs guard my steps.
Let Your torches show me the truth of myself,
Even when others turn away.

Let Your presence remind me:
My queerness is not a curse. It is a crossroads.
A holy place. A meeting ground of spirit and flesh,
Of love beyond law, of beauty beyond binaries.

I offer You my truth, unhidden.
I offer You my pride, hard-earned.
I offer You my wounds, still healing.
And I ask in return:

Grant me the courage to live fully.
The strength to walk alone when I must.
The wisdom to love myself in the face of rejection.
And the fire to protect those who still tremble in the dark.

HECATE AND MODERN SOCIAL MAGIC

Hecate is not just a goddess for solitary nights or quiet spells. She is a goddess of power, of justice, of fire in the face of fear. When we look at the world today—at injustice, inequality, and harm—we can feel her rising. She calls to witches, healers, and rebels not only to protect themselves, but to protect each other. Hecate's magic can be personal, but it is also political.

In ancient myths, Hecate stood apart from the other gods. She kept her sovereignty. She helped Demeter search for Persephone, not out of obligation, but out of compassion. She moved through the worlds as she pleased, answering to no one. For those of us working toward a better world, this is more than a story—it's a blueprint.

Social magic is the use of spiritual practice to support collective change. It means we use our tools—candles, prayers, spells, energy, intuition—not only for personal healing, but for community protection and justice. Hecate, with her torches and keys, is a natural guide in this work.

Imagine lighting a candle for missing women whose stories have gone unheard. Imagine leaving an offering at a crossroads and asking Hecate to bless those who are marching, protesting, voting, or organizing. Imagine calling on her during a spell to break cycles of violence, to uplift marginalized voices, to open the way for change.

This is not about making magic instead of action. It is magic *with* action. It is lighting a candle and making a phone call. Saying a prayer and showing up for a neighbor. Casting a spell and casting a vote. With Hecate, one does not replace the other—they walk hand in hand.

In protective magic, Hecate is fierce. You can call on her to help shield protesters, to guard activists, or to surround someone facing harm with invisible strength. A simple protection chant might be:

"Hecate, stand at the gate. Guard the brave. Dismantle hate. Torch in hand, hounds by side, Keep the truth on freedom's tide."

Write names or causes on paper and place them under a key on your altar. Light a black candle and ask Hecate to watch over them. Leave offerings—garlic, wine, or coins—at a crossroads in her honor.

Justice work is also part of her domain. You can work with her to expose lies, to call out abusers, or to bring peace to communities in pain. Some witches use mirror spells to reflect harm back to the source. Others write petitions and burn them under her moon, asking for healing and truth.

If you've ever been told you're too loud, too angry, too queer, too soft, too much—Hecate is your ally. She reminds you that your voice is sacred. That your boundaries are spells. That claiming your space is an act of power.

And she reminds us that collective magic is stronger. Circles of witches can call on her together, raising energy for housing justice, racial equity, gender freedom, or disability rights. Her torch can light many fires at once.

If you want to bring Hecate into your social magic practice, here are a few ways to begin:

- Create a justice altar with her image, a candle, and symbols of the cause you care about.
- Call on her before community meetings, protests, or rituals.
- Write invocations or chants that speak her name alongside your goals.
- Work with others to create rituals for healing and resistance.
- Leave offerings in her honor for those who fight for what's right.

Hecate is not neutral. She walks with the outcast, the survivor, the truth-teller. She walks with those who protect the vulnerable and those who dare to break the silence. She does not shrink from the hard things. She meets them with open eyes and steady hands.

When we say her name in our social magic, we are calling on all her power—not just for ourselves, but for each other. We are saying: the world can change. And we will help it do so.
She does not ask for perfection. She asks for heart. She asks for courage. And she shows up when we do.

Hecate's Wheel

Hecate's Key

HECATE SPELLS AND RITUALS

Here are 50 spells for working with Hecate, each crafted for a distinct purpose. Every spell honors Her role as a liminal goddess—guardian of witches, keeper of keys, and mother of spirits. Each includes practical components rooted in folk magic: herbs, oils, stones, roots, and flame. These are devotional workings meant to be done with respect, not command.

KEY OF THE HIDDEN PATH (For Revealing What Is Obscured)

You'll Need: A skeleton key, mugwort, black candle, parchment, dragon's blood oil. Begin this spell at twilight or under a waning moon—times when secrets stir and shadows speak. Cleanse your space. Dress the black candle with dragon's blood oil and roll it in crushed mugwort. As you anoint it, whisper:

**"By blood of the dragon and leaf of the seer,
Let what is hidden draw near."**

On the parchment, write the situation or question that feels veiled, unclear, or tangled. Be honest—write with feeling, not just logic. Fold the paper once toward you, place the skeleton key on top of it, and then place both beneath the candle.

Light the candle and sit before it in stillness. Say:
**"Hecate, who sees what others turn from,
Revealer of the road,
Open the gate that fog has covered.
Let what lies beneath come forth.
Let truth move like smoke toward my eyes."**

Gaze into the flame and let your mind wander—not to overthink, but to listen. If visions, words, or emotions come, receive them without judgment. Let the candle burn down completely.

Once the flame dies, carry the key with you for the next seven days. Sleep with it near your head, or wear it around your neck if possible. It becomes a sacred link to Her sight, helping you perceive signs, feelings, and truths that may otherwise go unnoticed. Keep the folded paper for one full moon cycle, then burn it to seal the knowing.

THE WITCH'S FLAME (To Ignite Personal Power)

You'll Need: Red candle, cinnamon, ginger root, High John the Conqueror root, a pinch of sulfur

Begin this working on a waxing moon, when energy builds and grows. Carve your full name into the red candle, pressing each letter in with intention. Anoint it with ginger oil, then roll it in powdered cinnamon and crushed sulfur (be cautious—do this in a well-ventilated area and avoid direct inhalation).

Place the candle on your altar or work surface. Set the ginger root on one side, and the High John root on the other—fire and earth watching over the flame to come. Before lighting, hold your hands over the candle and say:

"I call on the fire within,
The voice I silenced,
The will I forgot.
Hecate, torchbearer, stand with me now."

Light the candle. As it burns, take a deep breath and sit before it. Say aloud:
"Awaken my fire.
Let no fear dim what You have lit.
Let courage rise through smoke and spark.

Let me remember who I am."

Spend at least fifteen minutes watching the flame. Feel the heat of the flame reflect the heat of your own potential. Visualize your body filling with red light, steady and powerful.

When the candle has burned down halfway, snuff it and save the rest for another day of power-building. Carry the High John root with you after the ritual—wrapped in red cloth if you like—as a charm of command and boldness. The ginger root can be buried beneath your doorstep to draw ongoing energy into your space.

Repeat this spell as needed during times of doubt, fatigue, or when preparing to step into a challenge. Let the Witch's Flame remind you: your power is not lost. It is waiting to be claimed.

THREE ROADS PROTECTION SPELL *(For Spiritual Defense)*

You'll Need: Three black stones, rue, garlic, black salt, olive oil
Anoint the stones with olive oil, then roll them in crushed rue, minced garlic, and black salt. Place them at your door in a triangle pattern. Say:

"Hecate of the Crossroads, ward this threshold. Let what means me harm lose its way."

UNBINDING AT THE CROSSROADS *(To Break Spiritual Ties or Past Attachments)*

You'll Need: Poppy seeds, lemon peel, scissors, a piece of red thread
Write the name of the person or pattern you're releasing on a slip of paper. Wrap it in lemon peel and tie with red thread. Sprinkle poppy seeds around it. Say:

"I cut the tie, I end the thread. Hecate, free me from what holds me back."
Cut the thread with scissors and bury the bundle far from home or at a literal crossroads.

HECATE'S LANTERN SPELL *(Spirit Communication)*

You'll Need: Purple candle, graveyard dirt, mugwort, bay leaf, amethyst
Dress the candle with mugwort-infused oil. Place it atop a dish with a sprinkle of graveyard dirt and a bay leaf. Sit with an amethyst in hand. Light the candle and say:

"Hecate Psychopompos, open the veil. Let only the wise and willing speak."
Listen with care. Record what comes.

BLOODROOT BINDING *(To Silence a Malicious Tongue)*

You'll Need: Bloodroot, black thread, white cloth, vinegar, jar
Place bloodroot in white cloth, wrap it tightly, and tie with black thread. Put it in a jar filled with vinegar. Say:

"By root and stone, by silence and bone, Hecate, bind this bitter tongue."
Keep hidden and shake when activity stirs again. Dispose respectfully when no longer needed.

THE MIRROR OF TRUTH (For Self-Reflection and Shadow Work)

You'll Need: Obsidian mirror (or small black mirror), dried lavender, dried vervain, frankincense resin, charcoal disc, journal

Begin this ritual during the waning moon, a time when illusions dissolve and the truth beneath begins to surface. Cleanse your space with smoke, water, or prayer. Light the charcoal disc in a heatproof dish and place a pinch of frankincense resin onto it. As the fragrant smoke rises, place the mirror before you, and surround it with a ring of lavender and vervain.

Sit quietly and breathe deeply. Let the smoke veil your vision lightly. Speak aloud:
**"Hecate, torch in hand, show me the truth behind my mask.
What I fear, let me face.
What I've hidden, let me hold.
Guide me through my own shadows, without shame."**

Gaze into the mirror—not to see the future, but to meet your own eyes. This is not a time for judgment, but for deep listening. Let thoughts, memories, or emotions arise. If tears come, let them. If nothing comes, that too is part of the path.

Remain with the mirror for at least 15 minutes. When you're done, extinguish the charcoal safely and gather the herbs. Store them in a small pouch, and place it on your altar as a symbol of what you're learning to face. Journal everything that surfaced, even if it feels incomplete or unclear. Return to the mirror again during the next waning moon to continue the work.

HECATE'S KISS (For Queer Love and Authentic Affection)

You'll Need: Rose petals, pink candle, dried damiana, jasmine oil, a personal token (photo, piece of jewelry, letter, etc.)

Choose a quiet space where you can speak freely and be fully yourself. Dress the pink candle with jasmine oil, then roll it in crushed damiana and rose petals. As you do, speak softly: **"With love, not shame. With desire, not silence. This is holy."**

Place the token beside the candle—something that carries your truth, your longing, your queerness. This may be a memory, a dream, or a living connection. Light the candle and say:

**"Goddess of in-between hearts,
Bless the love that dares to live.
Bless the flame that burns outside the lines.
Let love rise in its true form—raw, radiant, and real."**

Spend a few moments speaking your truth aloud. Say what you want. Say what hurt. Say what you are still seeking. Let your voice be heard—not just by Hecate, but by your own heart.

Allow the candle to burn for 30 minutes. Snuff it safely and relight it each night for three nights, returning to your truth each time. After the final night, wrap your token in a piece of red or pink cloth and place it on your altar or near your bed. This becomes a charm for love in all its authentic forms—chosen, claimed, and honored.

Repeat this ritual when healing heartbreak, calling new love, or reclaiming yourself after rejection or shame.

THE CRONE'S DOOR (To Welcome Wise Dreams)

You'll Need: Dried mullein leaf, dried lavender, small fabric bag, moonstone, glass of water, white candle

Perform this spell in the evening, no later than one hour before bed. Place the herbs and moonstone into the fabric bag, tying it shut with intention. Hold it in your hands as you light the white candle beside your bed.

Say aloud:
"Crone of the night roads, walker between veils,
Guide me as I sleep.
Let dreams speak in symbols and spirit.
Let wisdom come soft and clear."

Pass the charm bag slowly through the candle's light three times, then place it above your bed or under your pillow. Set the glass of water nearby to absorb wandering energies or messages as you sleep.

Lie down and center yourself with three deep breaths. Whisper one question or request to Hecate before sleep—something you genuinely seek to understand. Allow your body to relax and surrender into Her keeping.

In the morning, before speaking to anyone or touching your phone, write down anything you remember from your dreams— words, symbols, emotions. Pay attention to patterns, even subtle ones. If nothing came, repeat the ritual for three consecutive nights.

Change the herbs in the charm bag every moon cycle to keep the work fresh. You may use the same moonstone again and again, as it continues to collect your dreaming.

This ritual may be especially helpful during liminal times— before major decisions, in grief, or when seeking deeper connection to the dead or your unconscious.

THE BONE PATH ROAD OPENER *(To Remove Obstacles)*

You'll Need: Chicken foot (cleaned), open roads oil, bay leaf, five-finger grass, yellow candle

Dress the candle in open roads oil. Wrap the bay leaf and five-finger grass around the chicken foot with red string. Say:

"Hecate, open the bone path. Let my steps be free and my way unbarred."
Burn the candle

THE CLOAK OF INVISIBILITY *(For Safety and Stealth)*

You'll Need: Poppy seed, agrimony, black cloth, myrrh oil, silver thread
 Dress the cloth with a dab of myrrh oil. Sew a small sachet with poppy seed and agrimony inside. Hold it to your chest and say:
 "Hecate, mask me from harm and hunger-eyes. Let me pass unnoticed, untouched, unseen."
 Carry when walking into unsafe spaces or difficult gatherings.

WITCH'S JUSTICE LAMP (For Righteous Justice and Setting Things Right)

You'll Need: Black candle, powdered sulfur, calamus root, devil's shoestring, iron nail, fireproof dish

Begin by cleansing your space, grounding yourself fully. You are entering sacred territory—the place where justice meets consequence. Dress the black candle with a dab of oil, then roll it in powdered sulfur. Place it in the center of the dish and create a circle of calamus root and devil's shoestring around it. Drive the iron nail firmly into the soil beside the candle.

Speak aloud:
 **"Hecate, hand of justice, wielder of unseen balance,
 Let what is crooked be straightened.
 Let what was stolen be returned or destroyed.
 Let the weight fall where it belongs."**

Light the candle and sit before it. Focus on the situation, not in hatred, but in honest remembrance. Allow Her flame to take your grief, anger, or sorrow—transmuting it into righteous heat. If this work is on behalf of another, name their truth, and ask for nothing you wouldn't accept yourself.

Let the candle burn to the end. When complete, bury the nail at a crossroads or near a boundary line. Dispose of herb remains respectfully. Know that you have spoken your truth to a goddess who does not forget.

TONGUES UNTIED (To Speak Your Truth Boldly)

You'll Need: Red candle, galangal root (chewing John), honey, parchment, pen

Find a quiet space where you won't be disturbed. On the parchment, write out what needs to be said—what your fear, silence, or shame has held back. Speak from the gut, not just the head. Anoint the red candle with honey, from base to wick, as you   say:
 "As sweet as truth, as sharp as fire, let my voice rise."

Light the candle and place it before you. Put the galangal root in your mouth and chew it gently, drawing power into your throat and belly. Say:

**"Hecate, loose my tongue that truth may rise like flame.
Let fear break. Let silence break. Let lies break."**

Speak aloud the words you wrote, or improvise from the heart. Say what you would say if the world were not watching. When done, spit the root into your hand and bury it at a crossroads or beneath a stone. Keep the parchment in a red cloth if the work continues—or burn it to release your voice into the world.

ANCESTRAL OFFERING SPELL (For Connection and Peace with the Dead)

You'll Need: White candle, graveyard dirt (collected respectfully), dried rosemary, black coffee, photo or heirloom of ancestor

This working is best done at dusk or midnight, when the veil is soft. Create a simple altar—place the ancestor's image or item in the center, the candle behind it, a line of graveyard dirt before it, and a cup of fresh black coffee nearby. Sprinkle rosemary around the image. Light the candle and say:

**"Hecate Psychopompos, guide the voices of my blood.
Open the road from shadow to flame.
Let the dead walk in peace. Let the living listen."**

Sit and speak to them. Tell them what's on your heart, or simply sit and wait. Watch the candle. Listen to the silence. If emotion rises, allow it.

Once the candle has burned halfway and the coffee has cooled, pour the coffee into the earth or at the roots of a tree. Bury the rosemary and dirt nearby. Repeat this ritual during Samhain, family anniversaries, or when the dead are restless or forgotten.

THE IRON LOCK (To End a Cycle or Bad Habit)

You'll Need: Rusty padlock, black string, vinegar, clove, small jar, parchment

This spell marks the sealing of a pattern—the final closing of a door that's trapped you. Begin by writing the habit, cycle, or pattern clearly on the parchment. Wrap the paper tightly around a clove, tying it with black string as you say:
"This binds me no more."

Fill a small jar halfway with vinegar. Drop the bundle into it, then drop in the padlock. As you seal the jar, say:
"Hecate, keyholder and lock-breaker,
Let this pattern be bound and drowned.
Let it lose its grip, and turn to ash in my blood."

Place the jar where it will not be disturbed. Each time you feel the old urge rise, shake the jar and say:
"You are sealed. I am free."

Once you feel the cycle has broken—whether in weeks or moons—bury the jar far from your home or at a crossroads, leaving a coin or herb as thanks.

HECATE'S CROWN OF LIGHT (For Wisdom in Times of Confusion)

You'll Need: Gold candle, bay laurel, dried chamomile, clear quartz, white cloth

Create a circle of bay and chamomile on a white cloth. Place the gold candle and quartz at the center. Sit quietly and breathe deeply. Light the candle and say:
"Hecate, crown of stars,
Illuminate the fog that clouds my mind.
Let Your fire rise in my spirit.
Let wisdom fall like ash from the heavens."

Hold the quartz in your hand and gaze into the candle flame. Focus on the issue that confuses you, the question you cannot answer. Let thoughts come and go. Don't chase. Don't force. Just listen.

When the candle has burned a while, snuff it and place the quartz under your pillow. Keep the herbs on your altar until clarity arrives. Repeat nightly as needed. Journal every message, no matter how small.

SPELL OF THE MIDNIGHT GATE (To Mark a Life Transition)

You'll Need: Three candles (white, black, grey), ashes (from burned herbs or paper), rose petals, small key, fireproof dish

This ritual should be done in solitude, preferably on the dark moon. Set the three candles in a triangle around a fireproof dish. In the dish, mix the ashes and rose petals. Place the key in the center.

Light the candles one by one, saying:
"White for what was.
Grey for what is.
Black for what must be."

Stand or kneel before the altar and speak aloud:
"I pass through, no longer who I was.
Let the dead self rest.
Let the new self rise.
Hecate, walk with me into what will be."

Sit in silence for as long as needed. When the candles burn out, wrap the key in black cloth and carry it with you as a token of passage. Bury the ashes and petals at a boundary—a doorway, riverbank, or crossroads.

HOUND'S HOWL SPELL (To Call Protection from Spirits or Unseen Forces)

You'll Need: Dog hair (ethically collected), iron filings, crushed garlic, black salt, graveyard dirt, red thread, pouch

Mix the herbs, filings, and dirt together in a bowl. Speak over them:
  "By fang, by footfall, by sacred breath,
  Let Her hounds circle round me now."

Place the blend into the pouch. Tie it closed with red thread, knotting it three times. As you hold the pouch, say:
  "Hecate, with black hounds pacing the veil,
  Guard me where others cannot.
  Let no spirit pass who means me harm."

Wear or carry the pouch when entering spiritually heavy places, haunted ground, or ritual space. Renew the ingredients each season, and bury the old ones with respect.

THE SERPENT'S SHEDDING (For Letting Go of Shame or Guilt)

You'll Need: Naturally shed snakeskin, myrrh resin, lemon balm, white candle, fireproof dish

Burn the myrrh on a charcoal disc and let the smoke cleanse you. Place the snakeskin across your chest or in your hands.

Close your eyes and say:
  "I carry this not to forget, but to grow.
  Like the serpent, I do not hate the skin I shed.
  I thank it. And I move on."

Rub lemon balm across your heart, shoulders, or wherever the shame has lived in your body. Light the white candle and let it burn as long as you sit in reflection. When ready, place the snakeskin on your altar as a symbol of transformation.

You may burn or bury it when you feel fully free, or keep it as a holy relic of your healing.

ROAD TO THE UNDERWORLD *(For Deep Ancestor Work or Spirit Walking)*

You'll Need: Pomegranate seeds, black obsidian, patchouli, bone or antler
Place obsidian and bone in a circle with the seeds and patchouli in the center. Say:
"Hecate, guide me beneath the world, where bones remember and truth sleeps."
Use for meditation or during trancework. Close the circle with reverence.

THE SHADOW CHAIN *(To Reveal What You're Avoiding in Yourself)*

You'll Need: Black ribbon, mirror, ink, angelica root
Sit before the mirror with the angelica root in hand. Tie a knot in the ribbon for each fear or avoided truth you speak aloud. Say:
"Hecate, bearer of hard truths, show me what I must face."
Keep the ribbon on your altar until you're ready to unbind each knot.

THE TORCH'S BLESSING *(To Light the Way for a New Endeavor)*

You'll Need: Orange candle, sunflower petals, cinnamon, citrine
Dress the candle in cinnamon oil, roll in sunflower petals. Place citrine beneath it. Say:
"Torch of Hecate, light my steps. Let this path bloom bold and bright."

Burn a little each day as you begin your journey. Recharge as needed.

THE KEY THAT BINDS *(To Create a Sacred Pact with Hecate)*

You'll Need: Silver key, white string, pomegranate juice, parchment
Write your vow, offering, or promise to Her on the parchment. Wrap the key in white string soaked in pomegranate juice. Say:
 "Hecate, witness of oaths, let this bond be sealed in shadow and flame."
Keep the key on your altar or wear it as a charm of devotion.

THE SILENT WATCHER *(For Divination Before Sleep)*

You'll Need: Mugwort, lavender, black tourmaline, small black candle
Place herbs under your pillow and the candle with the stone on your nightstand. Say:
 "Hecate, seer of signs, open the gate of sleep. Let truth walk into my dreams."
Light the candle before bed. Snuff before sleep. Record your dreams each morning.

THE FORKED TONGUE SPELL *(To Protect Against Manipulation and Lies)*

You'll Need: Devil's bit, slippery elm, alum powder, red candle
Mix herbs and powder in a small dish. Burn the red candle above it while saying:
 "Hecate, sharp of speech, bind deceitful tongues before they reach me."
Blow out the candle and dispose of remains at a crossroads.

THE MOTHER'S GAZE *(For Emotional Healing and*

Self-Forgiveness)

You'll Need: Pink rose petals, honey, white candle, chalice of water

Float the rose petals in the water. Drizzle honey into it. Light the white candle and say:

"Mother of shadows, see me whole. Teach me to love what I once cursed."

Sip the water and rest. Repeat as needed during healing work.

TORCH IN THE MIRROR (To See a Truth You've Been Avoiding)

You'll Need: Black mirror or bowl of water, white candle, dried vervain, dried mint, fireproof dish

This ritual should be done in solitude, preferably during the waning moon when shadows speak more freely. Begin by cleansing the space around you. Light the white candle and place it in front of the mirror or bowl of water so that the flame reflects. Burn the vervain and mint in a fireproof dish to create smoke. Let it rise and curl through the air, softening the edges of what is known.

Sit quietly and let your breath settle. As the flame flickers and the smoke dances, say:

"Hecate, torchbearer,
Light my way through illusion.
Show me what I fear to face.
Let no truth be too dark for Your flame."

Gaze into the mirror or water—not to scry the future, but to witness what has been hidden in plain sight. This might be an emotion long buried, a pattern you've ignored, a wound left unspoken. Speak aloud what you see, naming it without shame or fear. In naming, you begin to disarm it.

Remain in this space for at least fifteen minutes, letting the vision, memory, or awareness unfold at its own pace. When done, extinguish the candle and thank Hecate for Her light. You may write what you've discovered in a journal, or burn a small slip of paper describing what you are releasing. The mirror becomes a sacred tool after this work—keep it covered until needed again.

SPELL OF THE THRESHOLD FLAME (For Blessing a New Home or Sacred Space)

You'll Need: Bay leaves, dried rosemary, three white candles, iron nail, fireproof dish

Before beginning, clean and prepare the space you wish to bless. This may be a new home, a new room, or a sacred space you've recently claimed. Set one white candle at each main threshold— front door, back door, and interior space if needed. In a fireproof dish, burn a handful of bay leaves and rosemary together. Their smoke blesses, cleanses, and drives out what should not linger.

Move clockwise through the space. At each doorway, pause and say:
"Hecate, keeper of the gate,
Bless this home and ward its bones.
Let no harm cross this line.
Let peace take root and power rise."

As you say this, pass the smoke through each threshold, letting it touch the frames, corners, and entryways. Let the candles burn for at least 30 minutes, anchoring the light in each passage. When finished, drive the iron nail into the top or side of the main entrance—out of sight if needed.

This nail becomes a warding charm, a silent sentinel. You may repeat the smoke blessing monthly or after guests leave, arguments occur, or the atmosphere shifts. If moving out, remove the nail and thank Hecate for Her guardianship.

THE ASHEN JAR (To Dispel Lingering Grief)

You'll Need: Ashes (from burned herbs, paper, or incense), dried rose petals, graveyard dirt (collected with respect), small glass jar with lid

This spell is not to banish grief, but to give it form, containment, and a place to rest. Begin by writing a letter to the grief you carry—whether from loss, betrayal, change, or silence. Burn the letter safely and collect its ashes. In a clean glass jar, place the dried rose petals, then the ashes, and then a small handful of graveyard dirt. These three together represent beauty, memory, and death—woven into one vessel.

Hold the sealed jar in both hands. Close your eyes and say:
"I name my grief.
I do not bury it—I place it in the hands of Hecate.
Let it rest where the dead are heard and the living may heal."

Place the jar on your altar, windowsill, or a safe, quiet place in your home. Speak to it when the ache rises. Cry near it if needed. Let it absorb what your body can no longer hold.

Keep the jar for one full moon cycle. At the end of the cycle, take it to a river, graveyard, forest, or crossroads and bury it with thanks. Leave a coin or herb as offering. If grief returns, you may create another jar—but never rush this spell. It moves at the pace of mourning, not magic.

THE TRIPLE FLAME SPELL (To Call on All Three Forms of Hecate)

You'll Need: Three candles (white for Maiden, red for Mother, black for Crone), dried yarrow, dried thyme, mugwort

This spell honors Hecate in Her triple form, invoking the full cycle of becoming, being, and release. Begin by cleansing your space and placing the three candles in a triangle: white at the top, red to the right, and black to the left. In the center, lay a circle of yarrow, thyme, and mugwort—herbs of insight, strength, and vision.

Sit quietly, breathing deeply, and reflect on where you are in your life's cycle. Light the white candle first, saying:
  "Maiden, spark of becoming—light my way with fearless wonder."
  Then light the red candle, saying:
  "Mother, heart of the flame—sustain me with wisdom and warmth."
  Finally, light the black candle, saying:
  "Crone, keeper of endings—teach me how to release and transform."
  Speak together:
  "Hecate Trioditis, be with me in every phase."

Spend time in meditation, journaling, or prayer with the flames burning. You may speak your current needs to each form. When finished, snuff the candles in reverse order and save the herbs for future workings. Repeat this spell at life changes, crossroads, or when you need balance.

SHADOW DOOR SPELL (To Break Through Personal Stagnation)

You'll Need: Dried dandelion root, patchouli oil, black candle, rusty key

Begin at dusk or during a waning moon. Dress the black candle with patchouli oil and place it in front of you. Hold the dandelion root in your left hand and the rusty key in your right.

As you light the candle, say:
  "Hecate, opener of doors, break the wall I've built. Let me move."

Close your eyes and imagine the feeling of stuckness—where it lives in your body, how long it has been there, what it has stopped you from doing. Name it aloud, then say:
"No more."

Pass the key and root through the candle's flame (carefully) and through the smoke. Then bury both in the earth, preferably at a crossroads or under a threshold stone, as you whisper:
"Let this door stay open. Let me walk through."

Follow with real-world action within 24 hours to honor the shift you've called in.

HECATE'S GIFT (To Empower Your Magic with Her Blessing)

You'll Need: Dragon's blood resin, orange candle, a magical tool or charm

Burn the dragon's blood resin on a charcoal disc in a fireproof container. Light the orange candle and place it near the tool or charm you wish to charge. Pass the object slowly through the smoke three times, saying:
"Hecate, flame in the dark, bless this tool with fire and purpose."

Then hold it over the candle's light—not in the flame, but close enough to feel the heat. Speak aloud your intention for this tool—what you want it to carry, to do, to become in your hands. Sit with it in meditation until you feel the energy settle and bond.

Leave the tool near the burning candle until the flame dies naturally or is safely snuffed. Store it on your altar or use it in future rituals with awareness—it now holds a living spark of Her flame.

THE BLADE THAT CUTS (To Sever Harmful Attachments)

You'll Need: Rusty knife, black thread, name paper, graveyard dirt

Write the name, habit, or spiritual attachment on the paper. Wrap it with black thread, winding slowly while saying:
 "I bind what has bound me. I name what has held me."

Place the bundle on the earth or in a dish of graveyard dirt. With firm intention, pierce it with the rusty blade and say:
 "Hecate, severer of ties, cut what binds me to sorrow and harm.
 Let this cord fall, and not return."

Leave the bundle buried in graveyard dirt for one full moon cycle. After the cycle ends, either leave it buried permanently or burn it to finalize the release. Carry iron or protective charms with you for a week after to prevent the energy from reattaching.

GUIDING LANTERN SPELL (To Find Direction When Lost)

You'll Need: Yellow candle, bay leaf, dried vervain, compass or crossroads drawing

Perform this spell on a Thursday or under a waxing moon for best results. Carve a simple crossroads into the side of the yellow candle. On your working surface, place the compass or a drawn crossroads and sprinkle bay and vervain around it.

Light the candle and say:
 **"Hecate, holder of the lantern,
 Shine Your light into my doubt.
 Turn me toward the road that is mine."**

Sit in front of the flame, holding the compass or touching the drawing. Let your mind drift—not aimlessly, but with the silent question: "Where do I go from here?" Images, thoughts, and sensations may come. Trust your body's signals.

When you feel clarity rise, write it down immediately. Carry the bay leaf with you until your path unfolds, and repeat the spell whenever the way becomes unclear again.

THE ROOT OF PROTECTION (For Ongoing Spiritual Protection)

You'll Need: High John the Conqueror root, red flannel cloth, ground cinnamon, sewing needle and thread

This charm works best when created during a waxing moon or on a Tuesday. Place the root in the center of the red flannel cloth. Sprinkle a pinch of cinnamon over it, saying:
 **"Root of power, fire of spice,
 Guard me from harm, from shadow, from vice."**

Fold the cloth into a pouch and sew it closed with red thread, making three firm knots. With each knot, say:
 **"Hecate, shield and staff,
 Guard my body and soul from harm."**

Carry this charm in your pocket, bra, or bag daily. Refresh it every month by placing it near a burning white candle and sprinkling fresh cinnamon inside. It is especially effective when paired with other protective rituals.

JAR OF SILENCE (To Mute Gossip and Harmful Talk)

You'll Need: Glass jar with lid, alum powder, black string, paper with names or phrases

Write the names, slander, or phrases causing harm on the paper. Wrap it in black string and place it in the jar. Sprinkle alum powder over it, saying:
 "Alum to seal, string to bind,
 Let these words fall deaf and blind."

Seal the jar tightly and shake it once. Then say:
 "Hecate, queen of justice, seal this tongue that wounds without cause.
 Let no harm return to me."

Store the jar in a dark, undisturbed place—such as a closet or beneath the bed. If the gossip persists, shake the jar again. If it ends and peace is restored, you may choose to bury the jar or bury only the contents, rinsing and reusing the jar if desired.

THE BRAID OF FATE (To Call Forth What Is Meant for You)

You'll Need: Red, black, and white thread, dried rosemary, moonstone. Sit in sacred space, perhaps during a new moon or after a cleansing bath. Begin braiding the three threads together, speaking aloud your desire—not just what you want, but what you are truly meant to have. As you braid, say:

"Red for passion, black for depth, white for clarity.
 Hecate, weaver of roads,
 Bind my path to what is mine by fate."

Once braided, tie the rosemary and moonstone into the end of the cord. Breathe onto the charm three times to seal it. Keep it on your altar or carry it with you until you feel the path has revealed itself. Afterward, hang it somewhere visible to honor the road you now walk.

OIL OF OPENING (To Remove Spiritual Blockages)

You'll Need: Olive oil, dried peppermint, lemongrass, drop of your own blood (optional)

Infuse the olive oil with peppermint and lemongrass under a full moon or for at least three days. If spiritually safe and meaningful, add a drop of your own blood—this act binds your intent with sacred will. Shake the bottle gently and hold it to your chest.

Say:
**"Hecate, opener of doors,
Let no fear block my feet.
Let no wound keep me from rising.
Let my spirit walk free."**

Anoint the soles of your feet and your forehead before important rituals, conversations, or acts of courage. This oil may also be used to dress candles or tools for unblockings. Store in a dark place and remake every six moons for continued potency.

MASK OF THE UNKNOWN (To Conceal Yourself Spiritually)

You'll Need: Mirror, charcoal, poppy seeds, black cloth
Hold the mirror over a candle flame, letting it blacken slightly. Sprinkle poppy seeds across it, then wrap it in the black cloth. Say:
"Hecate, mistress of shadows, cloak me from the eyes that seek my light."

Keep wrapped and hidden. Use only when needing magical concealment.

THE COIN THAT SPEAKS (To Bring Prosperity Through Ancestral Favor)

You'll Need: Silver coin, mugwort, dried apple, ancestor photo or item. Place the coin on the ancestor photo with mugwort and apple slices around it. Say:

"Hecate, guide of spirits, let the dead walk with me in blessing."
Leave the offering out overnight, then carry the coin in your wallet.

HERB OF TRUTH (To Expose Deceit or Self-Deception)

You'll Need: Basil, mint, blue candle, clear bowl of water
Place the herbs in the bowl. Light the candle beside it. Gaze into the water and say:
"Hecate, torchbearer, show me what I refuse to see."
Record what rises. Repeat as needed when confusion clouds your path.

THE STRING THAT BINDS JUSTICE (To Hold Someone Accountable Spiritually)

You'll Need: Black string, photo or name paper, poppy pods, rusty nail
Wrap the string around the name paper and poppy pods. Pierce it with the rusty nail. Say:
"Hecate, witness of deeds, bind this one to the weight of their actions."
Store in a dark jar until justice comes. Dispose of it with care.

GATE OF RETURN (To Call Back Lost Energy)

You'll Need: White candle, dried lavender, salt, small mirror

This spell is best performed during the waxing moon, when what was diminished can begin to grow again. Begin by creating a sacred circle on your altar or floor using salt mixed with dried lavender. As you lay the circle, move clockwise and say:

"By earth and flower, by wound and will,
Let what was lost return to fill."

Place the white candle and mirror in the center of the circle, positioning them so the flame will reflect in the glass. Light the candle and gaze softly into the mirror. See not your face, but the space within you that has gone dim—energy taken by grief, drained by others, lost in hardship, or forgotten in distraction.

Say aloud:
"Hecate, threshold keeper,
Bringer of spirits, gatherer of pieces,
Bring back what was taken from me.
What fled in fear, what was stolen in silence—
Call it home."

Breathe deeply. Let your breath become a rhythm of calling. With each inhale, imagine drawing your energy back from the corners of memory, from past lovers, old heartbreaks, abandoned dreams, or fractured self-belief. You may feel warmth, tears, or a settling sensation. Stay with it.

Allow the candle to burn to completion. When done, close the salt circle with gratitude and bury the lavender near your home or scatter it in moving water. Keep the mirror on your altar for the next full moon, facing inward to hold your reclaimed light.

THREAD OF RECONCILIATION (To Mend a Broken Relationship)

You'll Need: Pink thread, dried rose petals, sugar, photo or written name of the person

Before beginning, reflect deeply on the nature of the rupture—

whether from misunderstanding, time, betrayal, or fear. This spell does not erase wrongdoing, but softens the ground for healing. In a clean space, place the rose petals on the photo or name paper. Wrap them together gently with pink thread. As you do, speak slowly:

"Thread of care, thread of grace,
Wind around this hardened place.
Let memory open, let kindness mend,
Let the cold between us end."

Once wrapped, roll the bundle lightly in sugar, letting it coat the outside. Place it in a small dish or on a plate, and say:

"Hecate, mother of compassion,
Keeper of love that defies the world,
Soften what has hardened between us."

Place the charm on your altar or windowsill, somewhere it will catch light. Each day for seven days, speak their name aloud— once in offering, once in hope, once in peace. If your heart allows, send a message or prayer to them, even if only in spirit.

After seven days, bury the charm in soft soil, asking Hecate to keep watch over the bond. If the person returns, meet them with truth. If they don't, let this be the spell that frees you from bitterness and opens you to new connection.

THE DOG'S BLESSING (To Honor and Call Her Protection)

You'll Need: Dog hair (ethically collected), rosemary, small pouch, bone charm
Place all items in the pouch and say:

"Hecate, with hounds at heel, let Your watch be over me."
Wear when walking at night or traveling alone.

LIFTING THE VEIL (To See Through a Spiritual Illusion)

You'll Need: Mullein, black tourmaline, purple candle, a glass of moon water. Anoint your forehead with moon water. Burn the candle and inhale the mullein smoke gently. Say:

"Hecate, queen of mist and mystery, lift the veil that clouds my mind."
Meditate and let Her reveal what's beneath the illusion.

THE SEED THAT GROWS (To Manifest a New Beginning)

You'll Need: Pumpkin seed, cinnamon, honey, green cloth
Rub the seed with cinnamon and honey. Wrap in green cloth and hold it to your chest. Say:

"Hecate, granter of grace, let this seed grow into the life I seek."
Bury the bundle near your home or in a flowerpot.

THE ROAD OF SHADOWS (To Walk Through Fear)

You'll Need: Black candle, bowl of graveyard dirt, piece of obsidian, dried yarrow, red thread, a personal item that carries memory or fear. Begin this ritual at dusk. Place the bowl of graveyard dirt in front of you. Light the black candle behind it so the flame casts long shadows over the surface. Place the piece of obsidian in the dirt, then lay your personal item beside it. Wind the red thread around your hand as you speak aloud the fear or memory you wish to face—not to banish, but to understand.

Say:
**"Hecate, keeper of the dark road, I do not turn away.
Let me walk this fear like a path. Let the shadow teach me what I need to know."**

Sprinkle yarrow over the dirt and gently press the personal item into the bowl. Sit in silence, watching the flame and allowing any emotions to surface. When ready, untie the thread slowly and say:

"I walk on, wiser and unbound."

Bury the bowl's contents at the foot of a tree or crossroads before the next full moon. Carry the obsidian as a talisman for the strength you reclaimed.

THE ALTAR OF BONES (To Connect with Ancestral Spirits and Seek Their Blessing)

You'll Need: Three white candles, chicken bones or other clean animal bones, dried rosemary, photograph or item of ancestor, bowl of water, black cloth, small key

Prepare a space that feels quiet and sacred. Cover a table or floor with the black cloth and arrange the three candles in a triangle. Place the bones in the center, forming a small circle or wheel. Add the rosemary inside the circle. Place the photograph or item of your ancestor beside the bone wheel. Set the bowl of water before you as an offering. Light the candles, one by one, saying:

"By candle flame and bone, I call.
By memory and blood, I reach.
Hecate, Psychopompos, open the door."

Sit and speak to your ancestor—aloud or in silence. Ask questions, offer updates, seek wisdom. Let the air between you hold your conversation. When ready, place the small key in the water and say:

"Let what is locked be opened. Let what is broken be remembered."

Leave the altar overnight, letting the candles burn safely. In the morning, remove the key and carry it as a link to your ancestor's guidance. Bury the bones respectfully or return them to nature. Use this ritual during Samhain, dark moons, or times of grief and seeking.

THE TORCH AND THE THREAD (To Reclaim Lost Power After Betrayal or Heartbreak)

You'll Need: Red candle, piece of black fabric, rose thorns, rosemary, a needle, a strip of red cloth or ribbon, written letter describing what was taken from you

Begin by writing a letter—not to the person, but to your own spirit. Describe what was taken: trust, voice, joy, or part of your power. Place the letter on the black fabric. Add the rose thorns and a sprig of rosemary on top. Fold the fabric around it tightly and sew it closed with red thread. As you sew, say with each stitch:

"Hecate, guardian of the wounded,
 I bind what was broken into strength.
 I do not return it—I remake it,
 By flame, by root, by will."

Light the red candle and hold the bundle over the flame's warmth (not burning). Say:
 "Torchbearer, let the fire in me rise again."

Carry the bundle for seven days. On the eighth, unwrap it and burn the letter safely. Scatter the herbs in running water or bury them at the base of a tree. Keep the red thread as a charm of reclamation.

CONCLUSION

This book is not the end of your path with Hecate. It's just one of the many doorways she opens. She is a goddess of beginnings, endings, and everything in between. She doesn't ask you to be perfect. She doesn't expect you to have all the answers. She only asks that you show up with truth in your heart and courage in your bones.

Whether you met her at a crossroads, on a dark moon, in a moment of grief, or in the middle of your magic—remember this: she chose to show up for you. And you chose to meet her there. Let that be enough.

She is the one who walks beside witches, misfits, seekers, protectors, and those who live in-between. She is the one who stays when the room is silent. When the road is dark. When the question is big.

And when you reach the next threshold in your life— when something ends, and something else begins— you will find her there, holding the torch.

So walk on. Speak her name. Trust your own magic. And remember: you were never walking alone.

Papa Gee

BIBLIOGRAPHY

Allen, Sarah. *Hekate: Saviors, Mothers and Witches in Ancient Greece.* Oxford University Press. 2010.

Barrett, Kerri. *Invoking Hekate: A Temple of the Bones.* Avalonia Publishing. 2012.

Berg, Beverly Moon & Kasulis, Thomas P. *Mythical and Spiritual Aspects of the Triple Goddess.* University Press of America. 1990.

Bilardi, Paul. *Italian Folk Magic: Rue's Kitchen Witchery.* Red Wheel/Weiser. 2018.

Clarke, Emma Kathryn. *Witch: Unleashed. Untamed. Unapologetic.* Hay House. 2017.

Crawford, Trista Hendren. *Hekate: She Who Holds the Keys.* Girl God Books. 2022.

d'Este, Sorita. *Hekate: Liminal Rites – A Study of the rituals, magic and symbols of the torch-bearing Triple Goddess of the Crossroads.* Avalonia Publishing. 2009.

deMedeiros, Courtney Leigh. "Hekate's Modern Devotees: Reclaiming the Goddess of the Crossroads." *Journal of Contemporary Pagan Studies*, Vol. 11, No. 2, 2015.

Downing, Christine. *The Goddess: Mythological Images of the Feminine.* Crossroad Publishing Company. 1981.

Gibson, Marion. *Witchcraft: A History in Thirteen Trials.* Scribner. 2023.

Hutton, Ronald. *The Triumph of the Moon: A History of Modern Pagan Witchcraft.* Oxford University Press. 1999.

Johnston, Sarah Iles. *Hekate Soteira: A Study of Hekate's Roles in the Chaldean Oracles and Related Literature.* Scholars Press. 1990.

Kerenyi, Karl. *The Gods of the Greeks.* Thames and Hudson. 1951.

Mikalson, Jon D. *Ancient Greek Religion.* Blackwell Publishing. 2005.

Petropoulos, J. C. B. *Hekate in Early Greek Religion and Myth.* University of Athens Press. 2001.

Strmiska, Michael F. "Modern Paganism in World Cultures: Comparative Perspectives." ABC-CLIO. 2005.

www.ingramcontent.com/pod-product-compliance
Lightning Source LLC
Chambersburg PA
CBHW071532120626
46550CB00006B/2421